AF610556

Teresa the traveler
Life is an Adventure

I dedicate this book to my parents because without their support this trip would not have been possible...and I mean that literally...they gave me the money to go.

Pieces of a Larger Puzzle

I often think life is a giant puzzle with pieces scattered throughout the world. Some of us spend our entire lives searching them out and fitting them together in the hopes of getting a tiny glimpse at the bigger picture. Here are some of the pieces I found along the way …

Columbia – When you are feeling low on love give it and it will come back to you tenfold.

Peru – You never know where a dance party will break out.

Argentina – A sole mate teaches you how to love someone; a soul mate teaches you how to love everyone.

Chili – Life isn't about waiting for the storm to pass; it's about learning to dance in the rain…and in the mud.

Bolivia – I am not alone, there are Johnny Cash lovers all over the world.

Florida – Anything is possible is you believe… and you have NASA's budget.

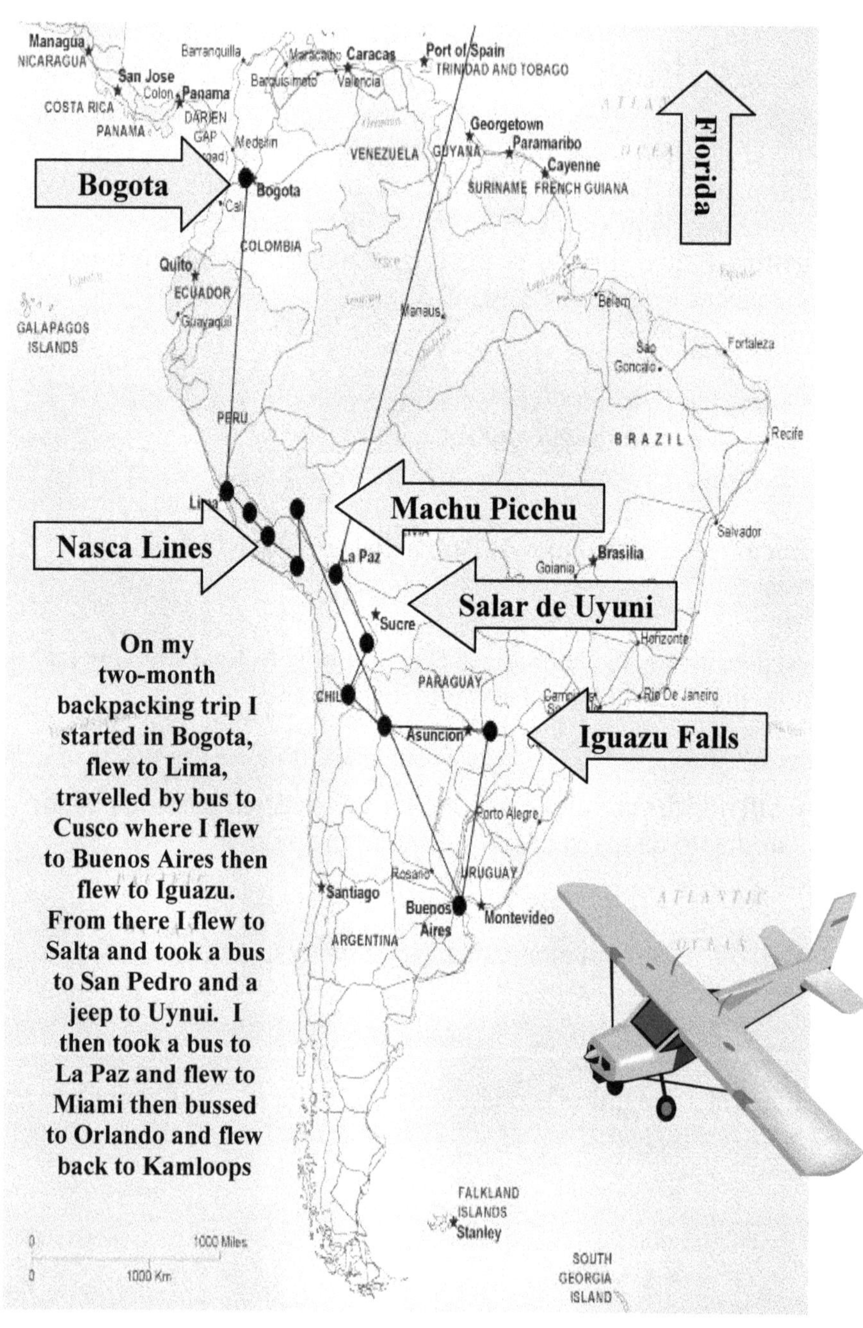

Bogota
Machu Picchu
Nasca Lines
Salar de Uyuni
Iguazu Falls
Florida
On my
two-month
backpacking trip I
started in Bogota,
flew to Lima,
travelled by bus to
Cusco where I flew
to Buenos Aires then
flew to Iguazu.
From there I flew to
Salta and took a bus
to San Pedro and a
jeep to Uynui. I
then took a bus to
La Paz and flew to
Miami then bussed
to Orlando and flew
back to Kamloops
Managua
NICARAGUA
San Jose
COSTA RICA
Colon
Panama
PANAMA
DARIEN
GAP
Barranquilla
Maracaibo
Caracas
Barquisimeto
Valencia
Port of Spain
TRINIDAD AND TOBAGO
Medellin
VENEZUELA
GUYANA
Georgetown
Paramaribo
Cayenne
SURINAME
FRENCH GUIANA
Bogota
Cali
COLOMBIA
Quito
ECUADOR
Guayaquil
GALAPAGOS
ISLANDS
Manaus
Belem
Fortaleza
Sao
Goncalo
PERU
BRAZIL
Recife
Lima
La Paz
Salvador
Brasilia
Goiania
Sucre
Horizonte
PARAGUAY
CHILE
Rio De Janeiro
Asuncion
Porto Alegre
Rosario
URUGUAY
Santiago
Buenos
Aires
Montevideo
ARGENTINA
FALKLAND
ISLANDS
Stanley
0
1000 Miles
0
1000 Km
SOUTH
GEORGIA
ISLAND

All photographs taken by Teresa Cline

(With the exception of the public domain pictures obtained from the Internet to illustrate historical background information)

Cover Page
By
Teresa Cline

Self-Published by
Teresa Cline
Kamloops, BC, Canada

teresathetraveler@hotmail.com

www.teresathetraveler.com

Special thanks to Wikipedia and Wikipedia Commons
For being a great resource for historical information.

Printed by Lulu
www.lulu.com

Follow Teresa The Traveler
on YouTube and Facebook

Soul Searching
In South America

TABLE OF CONTENTS

Winter of Discontent

June 8th 2010. I moved back to Kamloops in October of 2009 and had been living there for almost a year, a huge feat for someone who is not able to stay in one place for any length of time. And I mean that literally. I have a thing called restless leg syndrome and unless I am constantly on the move I feel like I have Charlie horses in both of my legs. Long international flights have always been a nightmare for me. I spend so much time pacing up and down the aisle I am surprised when the other passengers don't mistake me for a flight attendant.

For most people, a major accomplishment would be to leave their hometown for a year and travel somewhere new and exciting but I am not most people. For me a major accomplishment would be to stay put for an entire year and that is exactly what I did. Believe me it was not by choice. The Universe drove a large stake through my foot and said STAY. Not only was I unable to find another high paying camp job, a task that has never taken more than a month to achieve, I couldn't get there if I tried.

I also developed shin splints that prevented me from driving any longer than 30 minutes at a time and was also experiencing such stiffness in my knees that I could barely walk.

Aching to know why I was aching, I picked up my copy of *You Can Heal Your Life* and asked Louis Hay. She replied "Your stubborn ego and pride is causing your inability to bend. Not only are you overcome with fear, you are inflexible and won't give in. You need to break down your ideals and raise your standards in life".

What does she know?

To which she responded, if you don't believe me why do you refer to my book every time you stub your toe?

You are absolutely right, my apologies Mrs. Hay.

Why can't I just be where I am at?

Perhaps the Universe is only keeping me here until I let go of my ego, a term I am starting to believe is an acronym for Eluding God's Oneness. If I am really one with the world and everyone in it why do I feel so alone most of the time?

On the outside I come across as this confident successful woman who has traveled the world and has friends around the globe but the pathetic truth is that I spent most of the past year sitting alone in my townhouse with only my rabbit Jack to keep me company and believe me he is not a great conversationalist.

Oh yes, did I mention I bought a new townhouse and moved in at the beginning of December 2009?

I *was* living in a one-bedroom downtown condo and after having it on the market for over 8 months was relieved to be out of there. I prefer a quiet neighbourhood so why I moved into a noisy condo complex next to a crack house is beyond me.

I was sandwiched between two units full of deaf people; or if they weren't yet they would be if they continued listening to their music at full blast until the wee hours of the morning. Knocking on the door and asking them to turn it down was pointless because they couldn't hear me over Iron Maiden's Greatest Hits. Once I resorted to writing a note and sliding it under the door asking them to please keep it down but that didn't work either making me wonder if they were also illiterate.

I reached my breaking point when the comfortable-with-being-abused woman next door had an altercation with her jealous unemployed crack-head boyfriend. Upset that she went to a party without him, he took out his anger on the brand new high-end condo unit his girlfriend was renting. For over two hours I listened to him trash the place thinking he was doing some renovations.

At 11:00 pm, moments after I finally got to sleep, a nearly impossible feat for me ever since I returned from Afghanistan, I was awakened by a loud bang on my door. I threw on a robe, because I sleep in the buff, and let my neighbour in. She explained her conundrum and asked me to call the police, I agreed and she left. Moments later, she returned to tell me not to call the cops because she was going to call his mother to see if *she* could calm him down. I gave her a sure-whatever and called the police anyway. Any noisy crack-head who comes between me and a rendezvous with Mr. Sandman deserves a night in the drunk-tank.

Fifteen minutes later, two handsome young policemen arrived and I gladly buzzed them in and directed them to the neighbor's unit. While one tried to reason with the idiot next door, the other took statements from Miss "likely forgive him in the morning"...and from her daughter. Oh yes...did I mention her young teenage daughter is subject to this daily dysfunction? According to the mother, the daughter already has an abusive boyfriend. Big surprise!

Oh well, at least this dude is a step up from the previous loser she shared a home with. He stabbed her on the front lawn of their house leaving her for dead.

Never again will I buy a unit in a complex that allows rentals – renters tend to be kind people. The kind I would prefer not to share a building with.

I remember that glorious moment when I moved the last of my stuff out of the condo and handed the key to the young twenty-something guy who bought it. The first item he carried in was a large home stereo with a sub-woofer. I knew right away he was going to fit right in.

B-bye noisy condo!

▲ *I used to love winter but in the past few years I have not been a fan of the cold.*

I spent the next few months living between my parent's house and Albian Village in the oil sands where I worked.

On thanksgiving weekend of 2009, after four months of searching for my new abode, my realtor brought me to the perfect townhouse. Not only did it have a small storage room under the stairs for my rabbit Jack, it also had two bedrooms, one and a half bathrooms and a one-car garage. It was love at first sight!

I managed to get the place for twenty thousand less than the asking price because despite the wonderful layout, the bright yellow walls and dark blue kitchen screamed IKEA – a great place to shop but who wants to live there? The white cat-pee stained carpets and nineties-inspired gold and plastic crystal chandeliers also left a lot to be desired. I had my work cut out for me but I enjoy renovating so I was up to the challenge.

Excited to complete the purchase of my new abode, I returned to work to get a letter from my employer to satisfy the mortgage company. While waiting for the assistant to prepare it, I was laid off – a mere four hours after I had complained about being sexually harassed. Enraged that I lost my job while the man who harassed me remained gainfully employed I waged a human rights battle against the huge oil company and industrial construction company that allowed the injustice. A battle that continues to this day and most likely won't be solved anytime soon.

But I won't get into that since I already divulged all the details in my previous book, To Fort Mac and Back – Surviving the Alberta Oil Sands.

They say bad luck comes in threes and they (whoever they are) are absolutely right. In a period of one week, I not only lost my job, I got a three thousand dollar fine for driving an uninsured vehicle.

Unbeknownst to me, my insurance had expired and when I got stopped for speeding, my ticket turned into a court date three months later. To make matters worse, I got another speeding ticket on my way back to Edmonton for my court appearance.

Adding to my misery was the fact that my health was at an all time low. I had an incessant cough that would not allow me to sleep and I kept getting boils in the most bizarre locations. In a six-month period I got one in my nose, one in my ear and one on my lip. All three got infected and swelled up making my face look like I just received a George Foreman makeover.

I had to constantly remind myself that things would eventually work themselves out whether I worried about them or not – easier said than done for a woman who comes from a long line of worry warts.

Breathe Easy

Moving into my new townhouse was a godsend and spending the next four months renovating it kept my mind off being an unemployed, over-weight, and depressed single forty-year-old woman.

The other thing that worked in my favour was the fact that I was eligible to collect unemployment insurance for over a year. Because of the recession, the government had increased benefits for those who had not claimed EI in the past five or so years. As difficult as it was, the Universe seemed to be telling me to sit still for awhile and stop racing from job to job, man to man and country to country.

I remember the first time I forced myself to sit still when I was feeling restless. I was in a nightclub in Guatemala City with my friend Carolyn wishing I could be anywhere but where I was. I had quit smoking for over a month and this was my first time in bar without a cigarette in hand and I was starting to panic. As I stood there awkwardly with no one to talk to and nothing to do with my hands, a voice inside my head told me to, "Just feel awkward until you don't anymore."

Are you nuts? Who wants to stand in a bar by themselves feeling awkward?

But that is exactly what I did. Not because I was in the habit of listening to my inner voice but because I didn't have a cigarette to smoke and I couldn't find my friend to tell her I was leaving.

I just stood there noticing how uncomfortable I was until I didn't feel uncomfortable anymore.

Maybe what I needed to do was just sit with myself in one place until I was not uncomfortable with myself anymore. I had neglected me for too long that my body was screaming for me to take care of it. On New Year's Eve, after I returned home from a party at a friends' house, I promised to focus on regaining my health and asked the Universe for help in accomplishing the task.

It never ceases to amaze me how quickly the Universe responds to my greatest desires. My cough had gotten so bad that, not only was I kept awake all night; it hurt to cough because my chest was bruised from all the coughing. When I couldn't take it anymore I broke down on the bathroom floor sobbing frantically and screaming for the Universe to put an end to my misery.

Suddenly I started to wheeze and was barely able to get enough air to fill my lungs. I hopped into my car dressed in my pyjamas and bee-lined it to the emergency room. I was unable to speak so the admitting nurse rushed me to see a doctor who had me breathe a miracle mist that cleared my lungs making me feel better than I had in years.

I was finally diagnosed with Asthma, a condition that I have had my entire life but did not know. It was always misdiagnosed as bronchitis. Over the years I had taken so many rounds of antibiotics to clear up my "bronchitis" that I became immune to most of them.

I discovered I was allergic to dust mites that grow in carpets and my allergic reaction caused asthmatic attacks.

The little blue puffer of Ventolin that I took home from the hospital did wonders for my well-being. That loud, annoying, incessant cough that has plagued me since childhood was now a thing of the past.

First thing the following morning, I ripped out all the carpets in my townhouse and taught myself how to install laminate and vinyl flooring. Within ten days I had an allergen-free home.

Piano Woman

My new abode was perfect with the exception of one thing – the constant piano music that streamed into my living room from the unit next door. While it was a step up from the loud rock and roll music of the previous place, it was annoying just the same.

Upon meeting my new neighbour in the driveway I invited her in to see my place and in turn got a tour of her unit. When I saw she had a piano parked right up against our adjoining wall I knew right away what the culprit was. In an effort to alleviate the pesky piano I suggested she move it to the opposite wall even offering to pay her $200 for the inconvenience. She was concerned she may have to re-tune it after so I offered to cover the cost.

A procrastinator by nature, despite the fact she promised to move it she never did and instead provided me with a schedule so I would know when she was practicing. She also promised not to play past 7 pm. I tried to be out of the house during those hours but soon came to resent the fact that I was barely spending time in the new townhouse.

Playing the role of nice neighbour wasn't getting me far so I called her over and explained how frustrated I was with her piano playing and how every time I heard it I wanted to climb through the wall and tune it with a sledgehammer. I added that our combined effort to solve the matter seemed to be making it worse so I told her to play whenever she wanted and I would find a way to deal with it.

Later that day I went down to Future Shop and asked my favourite salesman to sell me a loud set of speakers complete with a sub-woofer. I set the speakers on the bookshelf that rested against our adjoining wall then downloaded 60 minutes of dance music with heavy base beats.

From then on, every time I heard annoying piano music trickle through the walls, I would play obnoxiously loud dance music and exercise by running up and down the stairs, which were also on our adjoining wall and no doubt sounded like a heard of wild elephants. I reasoned that if I did this two times a day for a few months I would be in terrific shape.

After five minutes I would turn off the stereo and much to my delight there would be no piano music.

My stair aerobics sessions went from a couple times a day to a couple times a week and within two months ended altogether. The speakers started to collect dust and my living room became a quiet retreat.

I recently ran into my neighbour in the backyard and she was pleased to inform me she had moved the piano to the other wall.

The whole ordeal taught me an important lesson. When someone is annoying you it is best to ignore them and make yourself happy.

Another thing I promised myself on New Year's Eve was that I would finally finish writing and editing my series of books.

I had been so busy in the past few years working and traveling and writing new books that I never managed to finish any of them. I had a series of six unfinished books sitting on my computer waiting for my attention. The task was overwhelming but I was determined to complete them before starting yet another. Inspired by Elizabeth Gilbert's book Eat, Pray, Love I added a new element to my books that I had not included in earlier drafts: me.

I wove stories of my own search for love and enlightenment into my tales of world travel which forced me to examine my life in a raw and vulnerable way. I wrote about all of my failed relationships with honesty that I had never before permitted myself and it wasn't easy. I was finally confronting my biggest fear: me. It was alarming to examine my own role in all the hurt I have been through in my life but I was ready to face my fears. My rabbit Jack had inspired me to do that.

Bad Old Putty Tat

Sometimes I think Jack is a Buddhist because he spends hours each day in a dark corner of his room under the stairs silently staring at the wall. He could give the Dali Lama a lesson on meditation. One evening Jack's sense of calm was threatened. He was out on the patio playing in the rabbit habitat I had made for him when I heard him frantically scratching at the door. I opened it and he scrambled into the living room almost wiping out on the laminate floor as he raced to his room under the stairs. He then sat outside his cage for the next hour loudly thumping to warn all the other neighbourhood rabbits of a predator. I wonder if Jack is aware of the fact that he is the only rabbit in the complex…probably not.

I looked outside to see what had scared him and I saw a cat lurking in the bushes. The patio is encased in chicken wire so there was no way the cat could have hurt Jack but I couldn't convince him of that.

Wanting to help my wimpy rabbit, I decided to teach him self-defence. First I inspired him, by showing him a couple clips of brave rabbits on YouTube. The first was one of a rabbit chasing a snake up a tree and the other was a scene from Monte Python of the small white killer rabbit who attacked and killed some knights. Then I taught him how to stand his ground and give the cat the evil eye and if that didn't work I showed him some kickboxing moves. Being a rabbit he has powerful back legs and could easily knockout any opponent.

The next day Jack was outside and I noticed the cat creeping around the patio checking him out. Way less scary in the daytime, the cat was no bigger than Jack and wore a cute red color with a tiny gold bell. I thought to myself, "You were scared of that? I thought you were a rabbit not a chicken!"

I opened the door to let him in but much to my delight he stayed where he was and held his ground giving the cat the evil eye. Then the cat lay down beside Jack on the other side of the chicken wire and the two just sat there getting used to each other.

I figured if Jack could face the bad old putty tat then I could face the ghosts of my past so day in and day out I woke up in the morning, walked down to the nearest Starbucks, wrote for two hours, came home, wrote for another two hours then walked back to the Starbucks in the evening and worked for a few more. The staff began to know me by name and started making my tall skinny hazelnut latte before I even got to the counter. I knew then it was time to expand my horizons so I started to frequent the other Starbucks as well.

During my long walks from coffee shop to coffee shop, I did something I hadn't done in years – shut up. I quieted my mind allowing myself to be completely in the moment and that is when I finally heard him…God. Over the past few years I had been so busy asking God a million questions that it never occurred to me to shut up long enough to let him answer. When I finally did he blurted out the answers so fast I started carrying a note pad to jot them all down. Perhaps he was afraid this window of opportunity would slam shut and wanted to impart as much information as he could before the inevitable.

Had I known all I had to do was sit still to find the answers, I could have saved a whack of cash on airfare and hotel rooms…but what fun would that be?

As I wrote about every humiliating dysfunctional relationship I have ever had, I started to notice a common thread: me. OMG – why did I keep doing this to myself? I deserved better than that. A wise man once told me, "We cannot change what we do not acknowledge" and I took his advice to heart. As difficult as it was, I started to examine the role I played and started to ask myself how I could do it differently.

Realizing I had set the bar pretty low, I acknowledged my tendency to fall in love with a man's potential rather than his actual. When I was treated badly, I often made excuses for the guy hoping that if I hung on long enough he would start treating me nice again. Why did I insist on sticking my head in the sand when it comes to seeing a man for who he really was?

I had completely lost faith in myself.

Of course dating hadn't been a problem since I got back from working in Afghanistan as I had been single for almost four years. With the exception of a few casual dates and a fling with a Turkish cave hotel owner in Cappadocia, the well had run dry.

When I looked in the mirror I could see why. I was a shell of my former self, the confidence had left my eyes and my usual long blond hair was an unflattering shade of brassy brown. My once shapely figure was draped in black cargo pants and a black t-shirt to hide that extra twenty pounds I insisted on carrying around.

I needed to change but how?

A few days later I received an email from Mitch – a divorced pilot I went high school with who literally swept me off my feet when he flew me over Kamloops in his private plane.

While he was a prince of a man that day, he had since played come here go away inviting me out then standing me up too many times to mention without feeling ashamed of how gullible I am. In my opinion he was an emotionally unavailable alcoholic yet despite my analysis, I immediately translated his first email in 6 months – that read something along the lines of "hey what's up" – as saying Teresa I love you.

While picking out my wedding dress and wondering who I should cut from the guest list to keep the cost down, Lady Gaga jumped into my head and started singing:

I want your love,
and I want your revenge
You and me could write a bad romance
I want your love
and all you love is revenge
You and me could write a bad romance

Oh-oh-oh-oh-oooh!
Oh-oh-oooh-oh-oh!
Caught in a bad romance

I mentally dragged the needle across the record until the music stopped. The last thing I needed was another bad romance so I hit delete – b-bye Mitch.

The Summer of Love

One of my ex-boyfriends married the love of his life in July and as a wedding present I offered to do all the photography. It was a beautiful wedding, everything about it from the stag to the shower to opening presents the following day was filled with love…something that had been missing from my life for way too long. How sad is that?

I was so busy focusing on my career and writing books that I completely neglected love. The growing pile of self-help books on my nightstand had been telling me this for some time but I refused to listen. I just looked at them and said, "Sure…what do you know?"

I wanted to give myself a big slap upside the head and say duh! OMG – I remember reading a warning on Facebook about people roaming the Earth who needed a slap upside the head.

I chuckled to myself thinking – I know plenty of them. It never occurred to me I was one. I really wanted a loving relationship with a good man but how could I expect a man to find me attractive when I didn't even find myself attractive?

I needed to make some changes in my life so I did what every woman does when she needs a change: I visited the hairdresser. Four hours later, with the help of a bottle of bleach, blond Teresa was back.

I hoped that lightening my hair would help me to lighten up and maybe even set me on the road to enlightenment.

Yes I know there is nothing in any Buddhist texts about going blonde as a means of achieving enlightenment but maybe that's just because they didn't have the bleaching technology that we do today.

▲ *Some fishermen try to catch some dinner while watching the sun set over Lundbom Lake*

A few days later I was struck with the sudden urge to buy a new wardrobe. For the past few years I had been wearing so much black that every time I entered a clothing store a customer would hand me something off the rack and ask if they could try it on. I would reply sure and hand it back to them curious as to why they needed *my* permission. It was only when my friend Maria got a job at a lingerie store in the mall and complained about having to wear all black to work that I finally understood.

The More We Get Together

As I started to feel better about myself I suddenly wanted to be friends with everyone. One night I couldn't sleep so I went onto Facebook and started randomly adding friends. I added friends of friends and complete strangers for no reason other than to meet new people. Before I knew it I had friends all over the world – Indonesia, Jordan, Saudi Arabia, England, France – you name it.

It reminded of the song *The More We Get Together* so I posted the YouTube video on my page to share with my new friends.

Oh, the more we get together,
Together, together,
Oh, the more we get together,
The happier we'll be.

For your friends are my friends,
And my friends are your friends.
Oh, the more we get together,
The happier we'll be!

My friend adding frenzy was rudely interrupted by the God of Facebook who blocked my account for two days and sent me this message: *Warning! You are engaging in behavior that may be considered annoying or abusive by other users. Facebook's systems determined that you were going too fast when adding friends. You must significantly slow down. Further misuse of site features may result in a temporary block or your account being permanently disabled.*

I stopped adding friends so I wouldn't get kicked off but that didn't seem to matter because in the next few days I started to get a ton of friend requests. Suddenly my list of Facebook Friends was growing faster than my library of how not to be a loser literature *and* my collection of failed relationships. I had so much fun befriending random people that my friend list quickly grew from around 500 to over a thousand in a matter of days. Perhaps it *was* okay to be friends with everyone.

Not everyone was happy with my decision to make new friends. In fact, one of my friends was so disturbed by the fact that I added some of "her friends" that she promptly sent me an email requesting I please ask her permission before doing such a ghastly thing again even going as far as hiding her friends list so no one could steal them in the future.

I felt bad and worried that my effort to expand my circle of friends was only going to piss people off. That is until I came across a fan page called shit my dad says and received a great piece of advice from this guy's father.

"Don't focus on the one guy who hates you. You don't go to the park and set your picnic down next to the only pile of dog shit."

However I couldn't blame her, a couple years ago a friend of mine added another friend of mine from Afghanistan and I was furious. I felt I had exclusive rights to my friends and I certainly wasn't going to share them with other friends – they could go find their OWN friends!

I also had a habit of deleting people from my friends list as though competing to win a prize for having the most exclusive friends list on Facebook. I remember how proud I was when I got it down to 200 – a respectable and manageable number of friends, family and acquaintances.

Always frustrated by how my friend Amber made friends with everyone, I wondered why she set no standards allowing anyone, no matter how damaged they were, to be her friend.

Thoughts such as "How could you be friends with that person? He has bad breath, she drinks too much, he has an annoying laugh – do these things not bother you?" often entered my mind. Apparently she was sometimes bothered by people's faults but she never let that deter her from hanging out with them. How un-North American. She reminded me of my friends from the Middle East where hanging out in a pack of less than ten is practically unheard of.

▲ *While camping at Lundbom Lake one weekend I spotted a couple of butterflies resting on a flower.*

My friend Jen once jokingly told me, there is not enough love in this world so when you find some, hang onto it tightly and whatever you do, don't share it! I laughed at the irony of it. Can a person really have too many friends? Too much love? At one time I would have answered a definite yes but now I was re-evaluating my position.

Joy was knocking at my heart but I was afraid to let it in. What if I did and then one day it left and I went back to feeling empty?

What was wrong with me? How was I coming up with this silly logic?

I Want to Know What Love Is

One night I was having coffee with my friend Mike and he asked what kind of man I was looking for. A few years back I would have pulled out a long list that included handsome, good career, sense of humour…you get the idea. But not anymore, I replied, "I want to be loved unconditionally". I no longer cared what he looked like, what he owned or if he liked to travel. I just wanted to be loved unconditionally – not that I even knew what that looked like but I was willing to find out.

As I drove home the song *I Want to Know What Love Is* by Foreigner came onto the radio.

I gotta take a little time
A little time to think things over
I better read between the lines
In case I need it when I'm older

Now this mountain I must climb
Feels like a world upon my shoulders
And through the clouds I see love shine
It keeps me warm as life grows colder

In my life there's been heartache and pain

I don't know if I can face it again
Can't stop now, I've traveled so far
To change this lonely life

I wanna know what love is
I want you to show me
I wanna feel what love is
I know you can show me

My eyes filled with tears as the words spoke right to my heart. At 40 years old, I had never been truly in love. I was no stranger to lust and infatuation but what I really wanted was that unconditional life changing love that makes you want to spend the rest of your life with another person. Was I was even capable of it? I hoped so.

A few days later I received an email from an old high school friend. He wrote that my ex Antonio, who has been divorced for two years, was in town and that I should call him. He also added that he recently finished medical school and was in his second year of residency at Queens University Hospital in Kingston, Ontario.

What the…? My ex who failed out of university was now a doctor. Was this the same guy who used to throw spaghetti out the window of his fourth floor apartment so he could watch it go splat on his neighbour's car?

My heart beat frantically. I wanted to call him but I was too scared because we had parted on such bad terms 20 years prior.

The number Joe gave me was for Antonio's parents house. I imagined calling and having his father answer the phone and tell me, you may not date my son, you are not Italian. How crazy is that? Twenty years later and I still remember Antonio telling me how his father said, "It is okay sleep with girls like Teresa but you should marry a nice Italian girl." How could those words hurt me as much today as they did back then?

Try as I may I could not force my finger to dial the number. Two days later the thought of seeing Antonio still weighed heavy on my mind. I wondered if he would be happy to see me, if he was still as handsome as I remembered and if all those feelings I had as a young woman would come flooding back.

Dying to see a picture of him, I searched Facebook and much to my delight found his profile; I sent him a tiny olive branch, a message that read "is this who I think it is". He replied the next day wanting to talk so I gave him my number and seconds later the phone rang…it was him.

I invited him for coffee offering to pick him up at his house – an address I hadn't been to for twenty years.

▲ *I dyed my hair blonde and started to dress sexier and my confidence started to return.*

My entire body shook as I pulled up to the house where he sat on his front steps waiting for me. My legs could barely propel me up the steps and into his open arms where he pulled me in for a hug that made me feel like we never parted.

He was nothing like I expected. His short hair and bodybuilder's physique was replaced by shoulder legs hair, a lean build and a more refined European look. He could not have looked more delicious and I could not have acted more inappropriately if I tried. Despite the fact like he looked more like Fabio than Hulk Hogan, I still saw him as the meathead who worked as a bouncer, spent hours pumping weights in the gym and dragged his knuckles using grunts as a means of communicating.

Most people have a filter between what they think and what they say, unfortunately I am not most people. As I sipped coffee across from this handsome doctor I blurted out, "A doctor…seriously? I figured you would become a prison warden or perhaps a common street thug. You hate people, why would you want to help them?"

If that wasn't bad enough, I confessed that I thought his father was a jerk for the advice he gave Antonio about marrying an Italian girl and went on to tell him that I didn't call him for fear his father would answer. He told me his father had passed away from a heart attack a year prior and I felt like a complete idiot. I could write an entire book on how to say the wrong things on a date but who would want to read it?

For reasons I don't understand, my inappropriate comments and social awkwardness did not send Antonio running in the opposite direction. In fact, he found my verbal diarrhoea rather enduring.

Was this guy for real? And to add to his perfect-ness, he wasn't the alcoholic, drug-addicted, unemployed man-whore that I often attracted. After a passionate one-week affair, Antonio returned to Kingston and I missed him like crazy so after a few weeks of talking on the phone three times a day, I couldn't be apart from him any longer and flew down to stay with him for a few weeks.

During this time, we took a mini-vacation to Ottawa. I had visited the parliament buildings with my family when I was 12 but had little recollection of the trip so I was excited to see them again. We parked by Byward Market near the Beaver Tail Stand. Antonio told me how the pastry had become famous during President Barak Obama's visit to Canada and he was dying to try one. As we stood on the street sharing a Beaver tail, he pulled me over to listen to a song that had come on over the loudspeaker claiming he loved the song. My heart skipped a beat when I heard *I Want to Know What Love Is* by Foreigner.

Center of the Universe

Despite the fact that things seemed to be going well in my life, I still cried myself to sleep every night completely unable to shake the depression I had been so bravely struggling with since my return from working in Afghanistan four years prior. Thankfully that was about to change but not until I reached the absolute depths of my despair.

One day while having coffee with my friend Mike, I threw out the question, "If you were a tourist in Kamloops what sites would you visit?" Being a snowboarder, he naturally named Sun Peaks then went on to add the Center of the Universe.

Huh? What are you talking about? He explained that in 1980, a man dressed in white robes arrived at Vidette Lake in Deadman Valley claiming to have found the Center of the Universe. The apprentice monk from San Francisco had been sent there by his master teacher who had pointed to a location on a map claiming it to be the spot.

The apprentice conducted a series of tests which produced positive results thus clearing the way for his Master Teacher's visit. Along with his entourage of followers, the Master completed his tests proclaiming the top of a grassy knoll overlooking Vidette Lake to be the real deal.

Monks believe that the Center of the Universe is an area where power lines intersect and one can find peace, or get centered, hence the name.

▲ *Visitor to the Center of the Universe often leave offerings on this altar.*

A number of markers were used to identify the area: it needed to be shaped like the prow of a ship and sloping to the South and supernatural occurrences like hearing the sound of singing and seeing fire with no source of ignition must also take place.

Curiosity peeked; I did an internet search and discovered the site was part of the Vidette Lake Resort, a small family owned wilderness camp so I called their toll free number and set up a tour. When I arrived at the gate, owner Ray Stad drove down on his quad to greet me inviting me for tea with his family. Over tea, his wife Ruth asked their daughter to bring out her dream board and the young girl produced a large green piece of cardboard with magazine clippings and words glued onto it. Ruth went on to explain how she had put this board together during a troubled time in her life then pointed to a small picture in the corner. It was the view of Vidette Lake from the Center of the Universe - the same picture I had seen in an online magazine.

I felt shivers run down my spine when she told me she had built the dream board three years prior to purchasing the Vidette Lake Resort – a place she had never even heard of at the time.

A few years after creating the dream board she received a phone call from a friend telling her to check out a resort for sale. Her and Ray purchased the resort shortly thereafter but it wasn't until a year later that Ruth realized it was the same place from her dream board.

Ray then brought me to the Center of the Universe - the reason for my journey. We walked through a gate and up a dirt road while Ray regaled me with tales of the various spiritual healers, native healers and monks he had met since moving there.

When we reached the grassy knoll, Ray took his shoes off then circled a large portal stone three times before entering the clearing – a ritual some Buddhist monks had taught him. I followed suit.

Upon entering the clearing we came upon a shrine where previous visitors had left offerings. Ray knew the stories behind almost every item pointing out a card blessed by the Dalai Lama, a cufflink with a red cross left by a Swiss doctor and a bracelet from a Canadian soldier who had served in Afghanistan. The black metal bracelet was engraved with the names of four soldiers along with the date December 30, 2009 and the words KPRT Kandahar, Afghanistan. The soldiers were Sergeant George Mick age 28 from Edmonton, Alberta, Sergeant Kirk Taylor age 28 from Yarmouth Nova Scotia, Corporal Zachery McCormack age 21 from Edmonton, Alberta and Private Garrette William Chidley age 21 from Cambridge, Ontario. All four soldiers were killed when their vehicle was struck by an IED in Kandahar City. Canadian journalist Michelle Lang reporting for the *Calgary Herald* was also killed in the blast.

According to Ray, the soldier had been struggling with Post Traumatic Stress Disorder (PTSD) and came to the Center of the Universe in search of healing. My eyes filled with tears. Between August 2006 and May 2007 I had worked for an American defense contractor as a maintenance electrician in Kandahar and Kabul. When I returned home life had gone on without me and I no longer felt as though I fit in. I had completely lost my ability to socialize and within two months had alienated myself from most of my friends. Not the same person I was before I had left, I found it easier to be alone and withdraw into a world of depression and isolation than put on the charade of being okay.

The next four years were some of the most difficult in my life, something was wrong with me but I had no idea what. Noisy crowds gave me panic attacks and the idea of meeting a group of friends at a pub scared me more than sitting in a bunker waiting out a Taliban rocket attack. My nights were spent waking up every hour then struggling to fall back into a fitful sleep.

It never occurred to me I might have Post Traumatic Stress Disorder because in my mind I had no right to suffer any ill effects from the war. I wasn't a soldier fighting for my country – I was simply an electrician there on my own free will to make some money. My life was never in danger, aside from the occasional rockets attack and one thwarted suicide bomb attack. My time in Afghanistan felt no different than living in a construction camp, something I had done for years.

Well maybe things were a bit different. I spent the occasional evening drinking coffee with the soldiers and medics listening to their combat stories. I remember talking to one medic friend whose unit was attacked by the enemy and he had the grizzly job of determining who to tend to first and who to leave for last because they were mostly likely beyond saving.

Not only did I feel pain for all the suffering going on around me by both soldiers and Afghans, I also struggled with feelings of guilt wondering if the "War was Just" as the keychain I purchased in Kandahar so boldly stated. Were we doing the right thing? Were we stopping terrorism or just being terrorists ourselves?

I longed to go back to the Middle East where I could fit in and even applied for jobs in Iraq and Kuwait but it wasn't meant to be, the Universe had other plans for me. Instead I found work in the Alberta Oils Sands as a Quality Control Inspector living in remote camps – a lifestyle that did not require me to be the old Teresa. What a relief.

However, my oil sands career was cut short after I complained about being harassed. I spent a year on unemployment insurance applying for every oil sand job available and getting nothing until I started to worry about how I was going to pay my mortgage.

Ray could see that I was in need of some healing so he brought me over to Turtle Rock, explaining that the Natives, who called this the Place of Life, believed the rock had magical healing powers.

Placing my feet in its v-shaped footholds I, strong independent Teresa Cline, for the first time in her life, admitted defeat. Then I asked the Universe for help.

When I returned home that night I researched Post Traumatic Stress Disorder and discovered compliments of Wikipedia that it is a *"severe anxiety disorder that can develop after exposure to any event that results in psychological trauma. This event may involve the threat of death to oneself or to someone else, or to one's own or someone else's physical, sexual, or psychological integrity, overwhelming the individual's ability to cope. As an effect of psychological trauma, PTSD is less frequent and more enduring than the more commonly seen acute stress response.*

Diagnostic symptoms for PTSD include re-experiencing the original trauma(s) through flashbacks or nightmares, avoidance of stimuli associated with the trauma, and increased arousal – such as difficulty falling or staying asleep, anger, and hypervigilance. Formal diagnostic criteria require that the symptoms last more than one month and cause significant impairment in social, occupational, or other important areas of functioning."

OMG...Welcome to my life.

As I further researched the subject I found an article by Steve Clemons in the Washington Note claiming that as of July 2010, "Approximately 300,000 returning Iraq and Afghanistan war vets -- a number equivalent to nearly 25% of America's active duty military -- suffer from post-traumatic stress disorder." According to a February 2010 article in the Hill Times Online by Tim Naumetz: "A total of 5,375 Canadian Forces veterans were receiving disability benefits for post-traumatic stress disorder as of last September." Was I just another statistic?

Dead Boyfriend Phobia

I was excited to tell Antonio about my experience but he never called that night. For the first time since we reconnected, Antonio didn't call and in the next few weeks his calls became fewer and farther between and the conversations we did have started to feel obligatory.

We had not even been together for two months and already we were drifting apart. I needed to know why? More importantly, I needed to know what I could do to make him love me.

I marched down to the bookstore and stocked up on relationship books hoping to learn everything I needed to know about winning a man's heart. I soon discovered that I was doing everything wrong. I was way too giving.

Of course I was. I grew up with a mother who, whenever I displeased her, told me I was selfish and never thought of anyone but myself. Naturally I began to believe it was wrong to put me first so I floundered through life seeking the approval of others, always putting their needs before mine until I became overburdened. I wanted to run away and often fantasized about faking my own death and moving to a place where I could take care of my own needs without feeling guilty. My over giving nature made my relationships with men a living nightmare. In my attempt to gain their approval and love I gave until I had nothing left to give. Then I would resent the guy for not giving back to me. Of course I never told them what I needed and was frustrated that they couldn't read my mind. Because of this, I was much happier when I was single and that is how I spent the majority of my first 40 years on the planet..

Unfortunately no self-help books could stop the train wreck in progress. Antonio finally quit calling altogether and I spent the next few days with a huge knot in my stomach hoping the phone would ring. I immediately assumed he either was sleeping with another woman or dead because those were the only reasons based on previous experience that I could come up with.

I know…how messed up is that?

My dead boyfriend phobia started when I was a child. Sometimes, rather than come home after work, my father would go drinking with his buddies and drive home in the middle of the night. Inundated with commercials warning about the dangers of drinking and driving, I would lay awake in bed waiting to hear his key unlock the door so I knew he was alive. Sometimes he didn't come home until two or three in the morning.

When I turned sixteen I got my license and remedied the problem by picking him up at the bar and driving him home myself assuming the role of parenting my parents.

That same year I got a job as a ski instructor at Tod Mountain where I met a handsome ski instructor named Kevin. We were the best of buddies and after the season ended he moved to Vancouver and we drifted apart. We reconnected at a party thrown by a mutual friend and Kevin asked for my phone number promising to take me on a date the following weekend. I sat by the phone waiting for his call but it never came. Feeling sad and rejected, my insecurities told me he probably met someone else and lost interest in me.

A year later I ran into a mutual friend who said, *what a shame about Kevin, eh?*

What do you mean?
You don't know?
Know what?
Kevin died.

He had fallen off a cliff that weekend. Crushed and feeling guilty for believing he was a jerk who stood me up, I wished I had known earlier so I could have gone to his funeral and properly grieved his passing.

Needless to say, I always got messed up when I didn't hear from a guy, often jumping to the assumption he was dead.

My fear of dead boyfriends worsened when I went to work in Afghanistan. They didn't call the Air Base in Kandahar Rocket City for nothing. For an entire month we had rocket attacks every other day. The military never kept us informed and we rarely found out if anyone got hurt.

My post rocket attack routine consisted of checking in with my work crew then waiting for my boyfriend Marcel to return my "are you okay?" text. The Roshan network that we relied on was not the most reliable and it could be hours before a text got through. I couldn't sleep until I got his reply. My time in Kandahar was filled with sleepless nights.

When I got transferred to a different camp we lost touch and our relationship ended. Then one day a female security guard from Kandahar transferred to my camp. She informed me that the helicopter Marcel managed had crashed and the entire crew died. I panicked wondering if Marcel was on that flight, despite the fact he was part of the ground crew and never flew in the helicopter. I emailed him to see if he was okay but he never responded, I called and texted but he never answered. I am not sure if he didn't respond because he was avoiding me or because he was dead.

Big Girls Don't Cry

After a week of beating myself up over everything I did wrong to ruin my relationship with Antonio, it suddenly occurred to me that I was reading the wrong books. I didn't need to know how to make Antonio love me. I needed to know how to make me love me. What was it going to take for me to finally love myself?

I read a quote that resonated with me, it said relinquishing all attachment may allow our relationship to return at a higher level or may permit someone better suited to us to come into our lives. But how do I do that? I was attached, I needed his love more than I needed air…or at least I thought I did.

Usually when the pain becomes more than I can handle I feed it with fatty foods, shopping or another relationship, but this time I was determined to do things differently.

After all, isn't the definition of insanity doing the same thing over and over but expecting different results?

With no relationship, food or shopping malls to fill the emptiness I had no choice but to be empty. I knew I needed to fill the space with self love but I was running a little low on that. I hated to admit it but the Universe was not giving me what I wanted: it was giving me what I needed.

On one of my daily hikes up to the lookout at Kenna Cartwright Park, Fergie came onto my MP3 player and sang her song *Big Girls Don't Cry* which seemed to sum up my situation.

The smell of your skin
lingers on me now
You're probably on your flight back
To your home town
I need some shelter of my own
protection, baby
To be with myself and center
Clarity, peace, serenity
I hope you know, I hope you know
That this has nothing to do with you
It's personal, myself and I
We've got some straightenin' out to do
And I'm gonna miss you
Like a child misses their blanket
But I've got to get a move on
with my life
It's time to be a big girl now
And big girls don't cry
Don't cry, don't cry, don't cry
The path that I'm walkin',
I must go alone
I must take the baby steps

'til I'm full grown, full grown
Fairy tales don't always have a
Happy ending, do they?
And I foresee the dark ahead if I stay

I had a long painful road ahead of me and didn't even know where to start. When I got home I called my friend Francine who encouraged me to sign up for Connections. They just happened to have a weekend retreat taking place in two weeks.

Learning to Connect

A number of my friends had attended such retreats in an effort to improve their relationship and communication skills, all returning with a more positive outlook on life. Being the strong independent woman I am, I thought I could fix myself by myself. It never occurred to me that in order to improve the way I connect with other people, I needed the help of other people. Duh!

The weekend started with me admitting to a group of complete strangers that despite the fact I looked so well put together and confident on the outside, I was a wreck on the inside. I had come there in an effort to change that. I wanted to be beautiful and confident inside and out.

Eyes filled with tears after admitting this horrible truth, I tried to compose myself for fear of appearing weak and vulnerable. Then I was reminded of something I heard at a lecture on meditation the week before: there is strength in vulnerability. How bizarre. As I stood there balling my eyes out and letting everyone see how vulnerable I was, I felt my strength coming back. Did accepting me unconditionally despite all my faults allow others to accept me unconditionally as well?

My partner for the weekend was a handsome 28-year old guy named Todd who had a striking resemblance to Antonio. After working through a number of emotionally charged exercises together and with the group, we sat in the lobby waiting for the room to be reassembled for the last part of the day. We had each been given a workbook and inside the cover was a list of songs to be played throughout the weekend. When I glossed over the song list my heart raced when I saw *I Want to Know What Love Is*. That song had fast become the anthem in my search for enlightenment.

As the final day was nearing its end I was disappointed that I still hadn't heard *my* song. Our final exercise consisted of a receiving line where one by one we walked through with our eyes closed and received love from the other participants. I was about four people away from my turn when *my* song came on. My heart flooded with emotion and my eyes welled up. While I was disappointed that it did not come on during my turn I was happy to hear it while giving love to others. Then, much to my surprise, the administrator, who had no idea about my attachment to the song, grabbed me by the arm and sent me through the line.

Over the weekend I had become so close to these people I was overwhelmed to hear my song while receiving their unconditional love. By the end of the weekend something had shifted inside me – I was finally starting to feel what love was. As I started to love myself a little more each day I found myself needing less medication. I went from taking allergy pills, asthma medication, anti-depressants, anti-inflammatory pills, restless leg medication, sleeping pills and anti-anxiety pills on a daily basis to requiring no medication at all. Best of all, the more centered I was, the easier it was for me to fall asleep at night – a luxury that did wonders for my well being. I knew I still had a ways to go but for the first time in over a year I could see light at the end of the tunnel – and it wasn't a train.

Let Go and Let GOD

In the weeks to come, magical things started to happen as the Universe taught me important lessons about patience and trust. I was shopping at London Drugs one day and needing to use the washroom but when I went to the customer service desk to get the key, I was informed that the bathroom was occupied.

As I stood there waiting (an activity that I absolutely hate) I was tempted to go back and say it was an emergency and ask for the key to the unoccupied men's room. But a little voice inside my head told me to do things differently.

I really didn't need to go that bad so there was no reason why I couldn't wait a few more minutes.

While I stood there impatiently trying to be patient, an old boyfriend Brian walked up to the service counter to return a DVD player. OMG, I hadn't seen him in years and had been thinking about him lately wondering what he was up to. I walked over and we gave each other a big hug.

Inside Out Leadership

Inside Out Leadership put on the retreat I attended and I recommend it to everyone. Here is an excerpt from their website:

The Connections retreat is your opportunity to challenge beliefs that are not working for you, learn ways to "do it differently" and start a powerful transformational experience in your life.

Our programs build on a foundation of personal development and experiential learning and promote greater self awareness with opportunities for each participant to uncover negative belief systems and challenge themselves to live a better life.

You will leave our programs with tools that will help you develop personal motivation, purpose and passion in your life, and improve your relationships.

Our leadership team is deeply committed to empowering people to live their lives with heart-felt purpose and passion. We're there for you during the experience and afterwards with follow-up and support.

Our conferences, retreats, and workshops are not static... you don't just sit and listen to a motivational speaker. Distinctive, experiential processes help you uncover hidden beliefs that block you from living the life you were meant to live.

For more information check them out at www.insideoutcanada.ca.

When I was 15 my family spent the summers camping at Adams Lake and that is where I met Brian. He lived on a nearby farm. My parents hated him because of his reputation for being nothing but trouble. He had totalled more than one vehicle and drank an unhealthy amount of whiskey. At night when he thought my parents were sleeping he would tap on the window of the camper where I slept and lure me out. My parents were furious when one night they caught me sneaking back into the camper drunk. They quickly moved me inside the cabin so they could keep a better eye on me.

One day, after totalling yet another vehicle, Brian got his friend George to give him a ride over to visit me. George was smitten and returned a few hours later, minus Brian, to bring me to a dance at the hall. When I questioned him as to Brian's whereabouts, he said Brian would meet us there.

While I spent the evening with George, who quickly became my new boyfriend, Brian, who had walked down to meet me, spent the evening with my parents licking his wounds over the fact his best friend stolen his girl.

I was happy to learn that Brian was married with two kids and opening up a new business so he could spend less time on the road as a trucker and more time with his family. As we parted I thanked the Universe for that valuable lesson in patience. I needed to be more patient and aware of my surroundings rather than frantically racing from one thing to the next. I needed to spend more time just being where I was and enjoying the moment. I have a picture on my wall that says we don't remember the days we remember the moments…how true!

My next important lesson came a few days later when I went for coffee at my favourite Starbucks only to discover that every table was taken. Usually I would leave and drive to another coffee shop but I really wanted to sit and have a coffee at that particular Starbucks.

Deciding to just trust things would work themselves out I stood in line and ordered a tall skinny hazelnut latte. I was almost at the front when I noticed a table free up. My first thought was to grab it then I noticed a couple behind me contemplating the same thing. I let them have it deciding not to buy into the notion of scarcity. Besides, I really wanted to sit at the table in front of the fireplace despite the fact there were two girls already sitting there. I got to the front of the line and ordered my coffee and as I stood there waiting for it, the two girls got up and left. I grabbed my coffee and sat down at my favorite table and thanked the Universe for once again taking care of things for me.

Coffee with a Sniper

Thankful for all the help the Universe had given me to assist with my Post Traumatic Stress Disorder; I still secretly wished I could meet someone who also had it so I could learn how to cope. I had gotten into the routine of meeting my business coach every Monday and noon at a coffee shop in North Kamloops called Cowboy Coffee. One particular Monday he failed to show up which, in the past, would have set me off. There is nothing I hate worse than getting stood up because then I have to deem that person untrustworthy and withdraw my love from them. Yes I am that messed up. Based on Jeremy's perfect track record I decided to cut him some slack and work on editing my book about Afghanistan. I was at the part where I attended the ramp ceremony for four fallen Canadian soldiers in Kandahar and I was thinking about how I would like to give a completed copy of the book to their families. However I did not know how to contact them.

At that moment a soldier in uniform walked past me to order a coffee so I asked him how to go about that and he promised to email me a contact number. I noticed a patch on the front of his jacket that said 2PPLC, the unit I had worked with during my stint in Bosnia in 2001 so I asked if he served there. He said yes, in a camp called Coralici – the same camp I worked at as a facilities maintenance manager. Then I asked him if he had been in the hot tub and much to my surprise, he said yes.

When I first got transferred to the camp in Coralici one of my friends told me about a hot tub that, according to rumour, some engineers had built. No one knew for sure if this luxury item actually existed because if the camp commander had ever caught wind of such shenanigans it would have surely been shut down. There were only ten members out of the over 200 man camp who belonged to the hot tub club and were privy to the location of the hidden key – I was one of them and much to my surprise so was this soldier. In fact, it was his unit that had built the tub out of a fireman's bladder, a sump pump from a tank, a submersible heater and a garbage can, in 1997. We became fast friends and when Jeremy finally showed up, the soldier and I committed to meeting for coffee at another time.

During our next coffee meeting he felt more comfortable talking about his past. Turns out he was close to retiring after a 30-year military career as a sniper. The guy has seen more shit than a diaper making him the poster child for Post Traumatic Stress Disorder and after years of counselling and therapy he now counsels others.

I hoped he could answer the question that had been praying on my mind since I got back from Afghanistan: How do you return to your old life and be normal after being in a war?

He replied, "You don't".

Wow, that made so much sense; I had spent the past three years trying to squish myself back into a box that I no longer fit into. Mr. Sniper gave me the permission to be who I was. Perhaps it's okay to insist a room has two secure escape routes, suck at making small talk, run for a shelter when I hear loud booms and struggle with anxiety and depression. Rather than strive to be normal, whatever that is, I needed to just accept my own shade of crazy and trust that people would like me just the way I was.

That night I promised to start trusting the Universe and as they say, let go and let God.

Faith is letting all your worries go because you know in your heart the Universe is working everything out for you - Teresa the Traveler

If I Make It Through December

December was a tough month. Still trying to get over Antonio, matters got even worse when our mutual friend informed me that he was in town. A part of me still hoped he would call and everything would be okay but I did my best to bitch slap that part and forget about him which wasn't easy.

His name haunted me. While booking a trip to Las Vegas a banner kept flashing across the screen that read fly to San Antonio. And when I visited the drop in clinic to get some immunization shots I had to sit through an entire interview with Antonio Banderas in the waiting room. When I got home I watched a documentary about a biker gang and the leader was named…you guessed it, Antonio. If the Universe was trying to tell me something I was not listening. I spent my days distracting myself and trying to convince myself that the man of my dreams was on his way but whenever I tried to picture him, Antonio's face always popped up. Go away!

By Christmas Eve I was so tired of unsuccessfully trying to forget him that I had a meltdown. I cried hysterically on the bathroom floor praying for the Universe to step in and give me a hand. At that very moment the phone rang. Unable to compose myself long enough to answer it, I let my answering machine pick up. The caller left a message:

Ho Ho Ho Merry Christmas this is Ray from the Center of the Universe…

That night I constructed a dream board as a means of focusing my desires so that the Universe knew what I wanted. I cut out pictures of couples in love, wedding pictures, wedding rings, romantic getaways, etc and glued them onto a piece of cardboard and hung it on my fridge. Seeing how it was Christmas Eve, I figured I would elicit the help of Santa Claus as well so I placed it under my Christmas tree. On Christmas day the phone rang: it was Antonio.

We had a perfectly pleasant conversation in which Antonio made absolutely no mention of why he failed to call for over two months. I was more confused than ever. I had assumed he lost interest and the relationship was over. Did he not get the memo that I was finally ready to get over him and move on? I guess not!

We arranged to meet for coffee the following day which caused a river of fear and anxiety to flood back into my body. I couldn't sleep a wink. As well, the pain in one of my legs returned making it difficult for me to walk. I immediately consulted my Louise Hay book to discover that my leg problem was caused by "Fear of the future. Not wanting to move".

No shit. I was deathly afraid of my near future. As desperately as I needed to know why he didn't call…and I mean desperate…I was also afraid to know the answer. What if his feelings for me were not as strong as my feelings for him? That would feel like death.

▲ *I gave Larry the Healing Tree a hug on my way to the Center of the Universe.*

Much to my surprise he brought his daughter along to meet me for coffee. Looking more handsome than ever he was quick to assure me he had spent the past few months working and going to the gym with his buddy and nothing else. He then gave me a big hug and kiss before pointing out the new necklace his daughter had bought him for Christmas.

I was relieved to see he was no longer sporting the crystal necklace. It kept falling into my mouth when we made love and when I asked him where he got it he replied it was a gift from an ex whom he was still in love with. There is nothing like a guy proclaiming his love for another woman to kill the mood in the bedroom.

My reaction to being with the two of them took me completely by surprise. It felt like home and my heart started to burst. I wanted more that anything to spend the rest of my life with these two. And that's when the trouble once again started. I wanted the relationship so bad I became attached to the idea and then I began to fear it wouldn't happen. I got myself worked up into a huge ball of stress.

All rational thoughts left my head making room for all the insecure thoughts to have a big party for the remainder of the holiday season. And believe me, they were a group of rowdy misfits worthy of a Jerry Springer episode.

Should Old Acquaintance be Forgot?

I had been feeling so good for the past month that I had stopped taking my herbal happy pills two weeks before Antonio returned to town. Bad move! Did I honestly think I would make it through the holidays without the help of Mr. 5-HTP and his buddy Valerian Root?

Amongst the things I needed to get over was my attachment to coping with my mental illness without the help of medication. While I simply refused to take anti-depressants I sometimes took herbal supplements. Trying to be ultra-independent and not rely on anyone or anything is probably what caused my depression in the first place.

I also needed to get over my shame. I was afraid people would judge me as being weak and mentally unstable. Worse yet, I was afraid that men would deem me unlovable if they found out. How ridiculous is that? The thing I want most in life is to find that wonderful man who would love me unconditionally yet I had already written myself off as being unworthy of love.

Although I fantasized about spending New Year's Eve going out for a romantic dinner with Antonio, having a steamy kiss at midnight then returning to my place to get reacquainted as lovers, the Universe had other plans. Antonio went out with his buddies and I went out with the girls to the Blue Grotto – a Kamloops nightclub that features live music. As I stood at the bar waiting to purchase my first of two drinks (I am a cheap drunk), a woman I had not seen in years came over and gave me a hug. I knew Denise from the crazy houseboating adventures I used to go on in my late twenties. She and her friends had an all-girl boat that we usually ran into at the annual beach parties held at the narrows every long weekend during the summer.

She had heard about my life as Teresa the Traveler and admired the fact I had published my own books. She wanted me to help her with a book she was writing about her experiences with depression – a topic she assumed I knew nothing about.

▲ *My friend Monique and I celebrated New Year's Day at Vidette Lake.*

When I learned she was there with her boyfriend of ten years, a high school friend of mine named Craig I went over to say hi. Craig told me about how he is always there to help Denise through her depression and how much he loves her for trusting him. They are each other's heroes. A few weeks prior, she couldn't take it anymore and reached out for help ending up in the hospital. Craig wanted to ensure she was getting the care she needed so he visited her regularly bringing along her favourite pyjamas and anything else he thought would make her more comfortable.

Their story brought tears to my eyes. Perhaps it was possible for a man to love a woman who suffers from depression and if that was the case, perhaps it was possible for a man to love me.

Larry the Healing Tree

It was important for me to do something significant on New Year's Day because I believe that what you do on the first day of the year sets the tone for the rest of the year. That is why Monique and I drove to the Center of the Universe to start the year on a spiritual note.

I guess this would be a good time to introduce you to my new BFF Monique the Mountain Biker. We were friends in junior high but lost touch after graduation and only recently reconnected on Facebook when we discovered we both had a passion for traveling.

Thankfully my two New Years Eve drinks didn't translate into a hangover because we headed out first thing in the morning picking up owner Ray Stad at his Savona home. How cool would it be to say you own the Center of the Universe? We arrived at Vidette Lake where the three of us parked along the dirt road and trekked up to the grassy knoll stopping along the way to hug Larry the healing tree. Yes, the tree is named Larry.

A few years ago a healer named Larry told Ray that this was a special tree because each branch symbolized one of his ancestors. As I hugged Larry I could feel his energy and it gave me a sense of calm. When I got to the healing rock I positioned my feet in the footholds and meditated. Along with asking for spiritual enlightenment, I also asked the Universe, once again, to help me find true love. They say the squeaky wheel always gets oiled first so I figured if I kept bugging the Universe my request would jump to the front of the line. After all, I was 42 and not getting any younger.

How pathetic is that? I still hadn't found true love at 42. I had only had three significant relationships in my life and they all occurred before I turned 21. My first boyfriend was a guy I met at Adams Lake when I was 15 and we dated on and off for a year. I met my second when I was almost 17. We made each other's lives miserable over a four year period.

And my third was Antonio. We met when I was 20 and he was 18. While he wasn't my first boyfriend, he was my other first. After dating for ten months we became intimate and despite the fact 21 is a healthy age to be sexually active, I was not your normal girl. I was deathly afraid of getting pregnant. I was certain that would ruin my life.

Yes, I believed having a baby would ruin my life. While so many of my friends dreamed of getting married and raising a family I dreaded the thought. I wanted to have a successful career and travel the world. The last thing I wanted was the white picket fence and 2.5 children. My life belonged to me, not to a litter of screaming children and a demanding husband with a receding hairline.

Perhaps that's why I kept my relationships short. Many of the guys I dated wanted to settle down and it just wasn't in my blood. I felt guilty not being able to give them what they wanted and ended up leaving a trail of broken hearts in my wake.

When I delivered the news to Antonio he was so devastated he drove four hours from Kamloops to Vancouver. He showed up on my doorstep in the middle of the night refusing to let it end. It bought us some more time but it wasn't meant to be. He met his now ex-wife and mother of his daughter a year later and spent the next 17 years happily married for the most part.

I spent the next twenty years at cross purposes with myself. While I wanted to be in a committed relationship, I also wanted to be free to do my own thing. I could never find a way to combine these two desires and at 42 years old I still couldn't. There must be a way to be in love and still be free follow your heart around the world.

My New Best Friend

Antonio's last night in town was a monumental disaster. Having barely spent any time with him during his stay I was desperate to spend some quality time with him before he left. I had been reading John Gray's book Men are From Mars Women are from Venus in an attempt to understand Antonio and hopefully communicate with him better. John told me to ask for the things I wanted and quit assuming guys will figure it out on their own... hmm...interesting. I really wanted Antonio to take me out to dinner on his last night but I felt ridiculous asking. I think like a typical girl and believe if he really loved me I shouldn't have to ask. Are men really that oblivious to the needs of women? My question was answered with lightning speed when I finally mustered up the courage to call Antonio and make my wish known.

He said he would think about it and get back to me. Then, since it was his second to last night in town, I asked if I could come over to his place to snuggle on the couch and watch a movie. He replied that he already had plans with his friend Joe – the same Joe he had spent most of his short time back in town with. I could barely hold back my tears while Antonio excitedly told me all about the new gaming system Joe just bought and how the two of them are going to be playing it all night. OMG…men really are that dumb!

I promptly ended the conversation saying I had to go to the coffee shop and work on my books then I hung up the phone and burst into tears. Why did I bother? This man was clearly not into me. How could he choose a stupid video game over time with me? Was I that boring? If I came with a joystick would he want me then?

The knot in my stomach grew to a painful size as I nervously waited for a dinner invitation. By 5pm when he still hadn't called I was devastated and cried yet another river of tears before deciding to take myself out to dinner. Just as I was walking out the door at 7pm the phone rang – it was Antonio. He left a message informing me that he was home. Good for him! It was too little too late. I reasoned if he really wanted to take me on a date he would have called earlier.

After a perfectly pleasant date with myself, I contemplated whether or not to return his call. What little self-esteem I had left told me he didn't deserve to see me so I waited it out.

Not wanting to wallow alone in my misery I called my mother to tell her I was upset – a move I seldom do out of fear she will try to fix me thus making me feel bad about feeling bad. She offered to come over and keep me company but I was too depressed to be a good hostess. I was deathly afraid that a visit from my mother would worsen my mood because we have had a strained relationship for as long as I can remember. I often feel judged like nothing I do is good enough while she often feels I get defensive and push her away. I always though mothers and daughters were supposed to be best friends but despite the fact we love each other the two of us seldom see eye to eye. I was starting to lose hope of us ever having a good relationship.

She insisted it was okay if I was lousy company and drove over to spend the night anyway. When she got there she did something she has never done before, she sat on the couch across from me and just let me be sad.

For the first time in my life she wasn't trying to fix me she was just letting me be me. She was being my friend and it felt great. As we chatted I confessed something that I had been hiding from her for years – I told her about being raped by my first boyfriend when I was fifteen. I kept it to myself for years because I was afraid she would blame herself. Her and my father had allowed him to spend the weekends at our house because he lived out of town. It was a relief to finally get it off my chest.

My mother helped me to calm down and told me I should call Antonio, which I finally did around 10:30 pm. He was happy to hear my voice yet was a bit baffled as to why it took so long for me to get back to him.

I told him I went out to dinner and he told me he ended up spending the evening with…yes you guessed it…Joe.

It was actually a relief when Antonio left town the following day. He promised to keep in touch with me over Facebook during my trip to South America but that remained to be seen. Oh ya…did I mention I was going on a two-month backpacking trip through South America?

After having spent over a year in Kamloops working on my books I was restless for adventure. All year I contemplated where I wanted to go and amongst the contenders were Asia and Africa and India but fate seemed to be pulling me south.

My mom cut out a newspaper article one day about a guy around my age named Kevin who, after getting diagnosed with a malignant brain tumor, decided to embark on a motorbike trip around the world. He started in Kamloops and was making his way to the tip of South America. He seemed like my kind of guy and I thought it would be cool to meet him.

Months later at a stagette party I started chatting with a girl who mentioned her boyfriend was back in town for a week. He was traveling in Central America on his motorbike. I asked if his name was Kevin and yes it was the same guy. She told him about me and he became a fan on my Facebook page and our friendship began. The next time he was in town, the three of us met for coffee and Kevin invited me to join him for a month in South America.

Around the same time my friend Jenifer introduced me to her husband Jeremy, a motivational speaker and leadership trainer. I started getting private coaching sessions from him in exchange for helping him launch his new Wow Leadership YouTube channel. When Jeremy mentioned he was going to Peru at the end of December for two weeks to participate in a project with a group called Developing World Connections, I thought it would be awesome to hook up with them so I could tell their story in my book.

With my unemployment insurance running out on January 1, 2011, my books all finished and no job prospects on the horizon, I decided to buy a one way ticket to Bogotá Columbia and start 2011 off with a bang. My word of 2011 was trust and what better way to learn trust than by meeting friends in a foreign country? Besides, I had to do something to keep myself busy until the spring when Antonio was back in town or I would drive myself crazy missing him. Or maybe the trip would help me get over my "boy head". I hate it when I am all messed up over a guy.

I was also hoping that this trip would help me gain back my self esteem because I was in short supply. As much as I loved Antonio, I was deathly afraid that I would let my insecurities ruin it. As things stood, I really had nothing better to do but set up a vigil around my phone waiting for him to call….I really needed to find a more productive hobby.

Why did I feel that I had to do everything right to make Antonio love me? Why couldn't I feel lovable just the way I was regardless of what Antonio felt? And if he wasn't able to love me unconditionally with all my flaws why couldn't I just go out and find someone who would? I needed to quit beating myself up and trust in my ability to attract a secure relationship into my life…but how? Perhaps my journey through South America would help me answer that question.

Lucky Penny

The day before I left on my trip I called my grandma to say goodbye. Fully expecting the fear-based advice she has given me in the past such as "don't drink the water or you'll get cancer", I braced myself for the worst. What would it be this time? Much to my surprise she told me she was proud of me for being brave enough to go on such an adventure by myself. My eyes welled up with tears never believing I would see the day when my grandma supported me unconditionally. It gave me hope.

After dropping Jack off with the rabbit sitter, I made one last ditch effort to purchase the perfect traveling jacket for my trip.

I had been looking for over a month for a stylish black nylon jacket at a reasonable price but to no avail. I stopped by Value Village hoping to find a used book to read on the plane when I was inspired to check out the jackets. A black windbreaker seemed to jump out at me so I tried it on and much to my delight it was a perfect fit and when I put my hands in the pockets I pulled out a Canadian penny heads up.

I believe in the superstition "find a penny pick it up through the day you will have good luck". In fact I collect all the Canadian pennies I find and put them in my travel backpack to give to people I meet in my travels. I tell them it will bring them luck and will also bring them to Canada one day.

I felt like the Universe was telling me I was on the right path and it was there to support me. I bought the $10 jacket and zipped the penny in the arm pocket for good luck.

▲ *Deadman Falls near Vidette Lake*

Don't run away from your problems...fly away.
Teresa the Traveler

Travel Tips: Before You Leave

Medical Insurance

Make sure you have travel medical insurance before you leave. Not every country has free universal medical and if you end up in a hospital it could cost you an arm and both legs. Insurance can be purchased online and through most banks and insurance companies.

Checked Luggage

If you are leaving from a small airport with a stopover at a major airport before leaving the country you will most likely need to claim your luggage at the major airport and clear customs. But don't worry, if you forget your luggage will go through customs on its own and meet you a week later.

Medications

Bring you medications from home as they are not the same quality in the South American pharmacies. For instance it is very difficult to find Sinutab and Tylenol for colds and the medications they have are not as effective.

American Money

Make sure that your American money does not have any rips or writing on it as the vendors will be reluctant to take it claiming the banks will not accept it in that condition.

It is also a good idea to keep a couple hundred American dollars with you at all times just in case the bank machine won't take your Visa.

Passports

Make a copy of your birth certificate and passport then email it to yourself so you have some ID if yours is lost or stolen. Leave your original birth certificate with a trusted family member as they will have to bring it to a passport office in Canada to get you a new one.

Toilet Paper and Tissue

The toilet paper and tissue in this area is of a very poor quality and barely adequate to wipe your butt or blow your nose with. You know how crappy 1-ply paper is? Well theirs is more like a half ply or quarter ply. If you have room I recommend bringing along a roll of 2-ply.

Immunization

There are a number of recommended and required shots and medications one needs to get before traveling to South America and they are not cheap. A full set could cost over $300. Be sure to get them at least a few weeks before you leave as you could experience cold and flu symptoms after getting them. Make sure to get a yellow fever shot if you are going to Brazil and be sure to have your certificate with you as they will not let you in the country without it.

Bogotá Blues

Thankfully my parents dropped me off at the airport 2 hours before my flight because, due to the poor winter conditions, my flight had been cancelled and I was rushed onto an earlier flight than mine that was just about to leave for Vancouver. With the help of my good friend Ativan (a tranquillizer) I was able to get some sleep on the four hour midnight flight to Toronto where I hopped on the 2 pm flight to Bogotá and sat on the tarmac for two and a half hours while the mechanics unsuccessfully attempted to repair the aircraft.

I was thankful to get off the plane and take a long nap on the floor of Pearson Airport before boarding a different flight at 11pm. I arrived in Bogotá on January 8th 2011 hoping that I had in fact booked a hotel room complete with a pick up from the airport. When I booked online they sent me a confirmation (at least that's what I think it was) in Spanish so I really had no clue if I had a ride or even a room. I was relieved to walk out of the airport and see a taxi driver holding a sign that read Teresa Cline.

▲ *Trams and uphill trains carry visitors to Monserrate on the mountain overlooking Bogota.*

It made up for the fact that my luggage was still in Toronto and would not make it too Columbia for another few days. I had no idea I was supposed to pick up my luggage in Toronto and go through customs. Dumb airport rules.

Now I had to make it through the next four days without toiletries, fresh clothes and worse of all fresh underwear. I wasn't about to wear it inside out on day two because that is just disgusting so I contemplated going commando until I could by a new pair. The first thing I did when I checked into the room was wash them in the sink…hmm…should I wear them wet?

It's probably a good thing I didn't get my luggage because my room was so small I don't think my suitcase would have fit anyways.

Learning to Make Due

I took a shower washed my hair with hand soap (not the greatest feeling) then took a five hour nap to lose my jet lag before venturing out on the town. Everything I needed was in my suitcase and I was feeling helpless without it, that is until I ventured into the slums of Bogotá and walked past a cobblestone street lined with people sleeping side by side on the cold sidewalk amongst the filth. Vendors working out of shops made from cardboard and canvas etched out a living in this harsh ghetto while Nelly Fertado sang *I'm like a Bird* over a boom box. The lyrics sent chills down my spine

I'm like a bird,
I'll only fly away
I don't know where my soul is,
I don't know where my home is

▲ *The cobblestone streets at the top of Monserrate are lined with shops and cafes.*

Wow, I felt like such a princess for complaining about having to wash my hair with hand soap as opposed to my favourite salon shampoo. I could not imagine having to live on the street, the scene really put my petty problems into perspective…thanks Universe. I needed a slap upside the head.

Mount Monserrate

The streets got even more dingy as I continued to walk downhill so I turned around to see if the upper part of the city was more beautiful. I noticed a cable car and a funicular (uphill tram) bringing people to the top of the hill overlooking Bogotá. Located at the top was a 17th century church with a shine devoted to "El Señor Caído" or the Fallen Lord. The hill serves as both a pilgrimage destination and tourist attraction. I rode the funicular to the top and checked out the church before browsing through the many shops and cafes. By this time my stomach was so empty t it was threatening to eat itself so I risked some local cuisine.

Since no one spoke English and the menus were all in Spanish, I sat there until a bowl of soup was delivered to the table next to me. I motioned for the waitress to bring me the same and was soon eating my first and last bowl of corn on the cob chicken potato soup.

Made from a bowl of potato broth with chucks of potato, half a cob of corn and a chicken drumstick, this tasteless concoction could not induce a starving man to clean his bowl. As I did my best to force at least some of it in my stomach, I couldn't help thinking that Bogotá might be the place for me to lose that last ten pounds. I paid my bill which came to $20,000 –Columbian pesos or $10 Canadian. I suck at math and having to deal in currency with that many zeros made my head hurt. I could never live in a country with ridiculously inflated currency.

With a half full tummy I made my way over to the terrace for a breathtaking view of Bogotá. The capital of Columbia is also its most populated city with an estimated 7,304,384 inhabitants. In terms of land mass it ranks as the 30th largest city in the world and one of the biggest in Latin America. It is also the third highest capital city in the world at 2625 meters above sea level.

Considered one of the world's most violent cities in the mid-90's, in 1993 there were 4,352 homicides at a rate of 81 per 100,000 people. Having gone to great lengths to control the crime rate, in 2007 the number dropped to 1,401 murders for a rate of 19 per 100,000 people. Despite the bad reputation Columbia gained in the 1980's and early 1990's, aggressive publicity campaigns and increased security have been put in place. As well, the District Institute of Tourism set the goal of making Bogotá a sustainable tourist destination.

Take me to your Virgin

Across the hills I spotted a huge statue of the Virgin Mary reminiscent of Rio's Christ the Redeemer. Wanting to see it close up, I took the tram back down and walked to the road that led up the mountain to it. I asked a policeman if it was possible for me to walk to the statue and he said no making slicing motions across his neck with their fingers. Not entirely sure what the policeman meant, I found an English speaking guide and asked him for clarification. He informed me that to hike to the statue I would have to pass through some dangerous areas where I could get my throat slit. Nice! He recommended I find a taxi driver, preferably one recommended by my hotel, to drive me there.

▲ *A young man enjoys the view over Bogotá.*

The following morning I did just that. I hired a young private driver named Mauricio to drive me up the long winding road to the top of Guadelupe Peak to get up close and personal with the 15-meter sculpture of the Virgin of the Immaculate Conception that stood on top of a small church. Apparently it is a place of pilgrimage for Columbia's Christian community.

▲ *A 15-meter sculpture of the Virgin of the Immaculate Conception was erected on Bogota's highest mountain peak Guadalupe.*

What kind of Bull is this?

From the viewpoint I spotted the stadium where Bogotá's bullfights take place and, in a combination of Pictionary and Charades, managed to ask my Spanish speaking guide to take me there.

Located in the Macarena district, the Plaza de Toros Santamaria was opened to the public in February 1931 and has since hosted many of the world's top bullfighters. Its short season runs from mid January to the end of February.

A traditional spectacle in such countries as Spain, Portugal, Mexico, Columbia, Peru, and Ecuador and in Central America, this blood sport is considered a fine art by its followers. The largest bullfighting venue (seating 48,000 spectators) is the Plaza de toros Mexico in Mexico City while the oldest is the La Maestranza in Sevilla Spain which hosted its first bull fight in 1765.

In Spanish style bullfighting, the style that takes place in Columbia, three matadors, with the assistance of two picadors, three banderilleros and a mozo de espadas, each fight two bulls.

Accompanied by band music, participants parade into the stadium, wearing 18th century inspired Andalusian clothing, and salute the presiding dignitary. The highly ritualized event takes place in three stages called tercious the start of which is announced by a bugle call.

The Lancing – During the first stage, the bull enters the ring and the matador performs a series of passes using a magenta and gold cape in order to observe the bulls behaviour and ferocity. Next a picador on horseback enters the arena and stabs the bull in the neck. The horse is covered with a padding to protect it from the bull's horns, however prior to 1930 this was not the case and the horse was usually disembowelled at this stage.

The Third of Banderillas – During the second stage, the three banderillas each attempt to insert two sharp barbed sticks or banderillas into the bull's shoulders. This act angers and invigorates the bull and further weakens it.

The Third of Death – During the third stage the matador enters the ring alone with a small red cape and a sword. Contrary to popular belief, the color red does not anger the colorblind bulls. Using the cape to attract the bull in a series of passes, the matador both wears the bull out and performs for the crowd. In order to demonstrate his domination over the beast he may hold the cape especially close to his body. During the final kill, the matador attempts to manoeuvre the bull into a position where he can stab it between the shoulder blades and through the heart in an act called an estocada.

If the matador has performed exceptionally well the crowd will wave white handkerchiefs petitioning the president to award him an ear of the bull. In the rare occasion that the crowd and matador believe the bull has put on a brave fight, they may even petition to spare his life and return to the ranch to live out his life as a stud bull.

The stadium was closed when we arrived but the caretakers were kind enough to let us in to view it. Workers were cleaning up the sandy ring in the center where small pools of blood were all that remained of the last bull to meet its makers for the entertainment of the blood thirsty crowd.

▲ *The Plaza de Toros Santamaria in Bogota is where the bullfighting takes place from mid January to the end of February.*

Juan Belmonte – *The Greatest Bullfighter of All Time*

Born in 1892 in Seville Spain, Juan Belmonte is thought by many to be the greatest bullfighter of all time. Because he was born with deformed legs, rather than dance around the bull like other matadors, he stood his ground always remaining within inches of the bull and frequently getting gored. He is accredited with changing the style of bullfighting.

He fought 109 corridas in 1919, a number not matched by any matador until 1965. But his fame came with a price and eventually his doctor told him he could no longer smoke cigars, ride horses, drink wine or have sex with women. Unwilling to live if he could not partake in his favorite activities, he rode his horse to his finca to spent one final night smoking cigars, drinking wine and having sex with two prostitutes before shooting himself with his own pistol.

Before his death he was quoted as saying if he could not live like a man he would die like one.

▲ *The main square in Zipaquira*

I don't know that I could handle seeing an actual bullfight. It seems like such a cruel way to kill an animal. In fact, a number of animal rights activists claim the bull suffers a slow and tortuous death and have called for an end to the spectacle. In 1899 Argentina banned bullfighting and in 1912 it was abolished by Uruguay but despite anti-bullfighting demonstrations throughout the world the tradition continues in many countries to this day.

Salt Cathedral

When he dropped me off at my hotel, my guide suggested I visit the Salt Cathedral in the nearby town of Zipaquira so I hired him to take me there the following day.

A 2-hour drive from Bogotá brought me to Zipaquira – one of the oldest cities in Columbia dating back to the Spanish conquest.

Built 200 meters underground in the Halite Mountain, the Salt Cathedral, which has no official status as a cathedral or even a bishop, is a functioning church attracting as many as 3000 visitors a day.

The Halite mines have been exploited since the 5th century but it wasn't until the 1930's when miners carved out a sanctuary to use as their place for daily prayers so they could ask the saints for protection before starting work. In 1950, construction of a larger cathedral had begun and in 1954 it was dedicated to Our Lady of Rosary, the patron saint of miners. It was shut down in 1990 due to safety concerns over structural problems and then reopened 285 million dollars worth of construction later.

The main sections of the building include the Stations of the Cross (14 small chapels illustrating Jesus' final journey), the Dome and the three naves symbolizing the birth and death of Jesus.

▲ *A carving of the Creation of Adam, the painting gracing the center of the Sistine Chapel adorns the floor of the chapel.*

Help I'm Drowning

Three days in Bogotá and Antonio still hadn't retuned my email making me an emotional wreck. This come here go away game was wreaking havoc on my heart. Was this a normal thing that couples must endure at the beginning of a relationship or was I just attracted to emotionally unavailable men? I felt so defeated and wondered how much more pain my heart could take. What is it about this love thing that I was not getting? I thought being in love was supposed to feel good but the deeper I fell the more depressed and anxious I became.

I read a quote on the internet that seemed to sum up my situation.

Anxiety is love's greatest killer. It makes others feel as you might when a drowning man holds on to you. You want to save him, but you know he will strangle you with his panic. - Anais Nin

▲ *A Guatemalan fortune teller spreads enlightenment on the streets of Bogotá.*

I think this Anais Nin dude must have had me in mind when he wrote this. That's probably why Antonio wanted nothing to do with me. He could sense my desperation and knew I was drowning. I don't blame him for not wanting to go under with me; there was nothing he could do to save me.

Perhaps he hadn't turned his back on me after all. Maybe he was just sitting on the shore hoping I'd remember how to swim. I guess only time would tell.

Soul Food

When I finally dried up the big horse tears that threatened to drown my face, I went out in search of dinner. There were a number of people begging on the streets which was hard for me to see because I wanted to give money to them all but if I did there would be none left for me. As difficult as it was, I had learned to look after my own needs first and only give to others what I had to spare.

I found a place that served chicken so I went in and ordered a chicken bean and rice platter. An old lady lingered around the door wanting money so I handed her a few pesos. She left then came back as though she needed more.

She reminded me of a lady I had met in Guatemala who approached me on the street asking for food. I had no food so I gave her money but she insisted she needed food because the restaurants would not let her in. It was hard to believe that a restaurant would deny a paying customer so I invited her to join me for lunch at a fast food joint. We sat down at a table and, much to my surprise, the waiter asked her to leave. I was stunned. The lady next to me quipped, "Can you believe that"? She was clearly referring to the fact that the homeless lady entered the restaurant. Needless to say, she was baffled when I replied, "I know I can't believe my friend just got kicked out".

I walked out and over to another fast food place where I stood at a counter and ordered for her while she stood on the street shouting out her request. I handed her two pieces of chicken, some fries and a coke then gave her some money and wished her well feeling awful that she had to beg for food in the first place.

I had a feeling that this lady was hungry as well so I had the waiter wrap up my leftovers and I handed them to her on my way out. Her face lit up and she said something in Spanish, probably thank you.

As I continued down the street I noticed an old man sitting on the sidewalk asking for change *(and not the kind President Obama asked for during his campaign).* I had no more money to give so instead I gave him love; heaven knows we could all use some of that. I smiled and waved at him and in my mind I wished him well. He smiled and waved back saying thanks.

My mood started to lift and my pity party ended, at least for the moment. I put on my MP3 player and on came a bluegrass version of Amazing Grace. I sang along in my head, at least I think it was only in my head, and enjoyed people watching on the bustling main street when a fortune teller caught my eye.

I obviously needed a little spiritual advice so I hesitated as I approached him. Looking at the small table he had set up I asked if he spoke English. Much to my surprise he did. Born in Guatemala he was raised in San Francisco and had lived in countless countries including Holland, Haiti and Cuba. He had a calm energy about him and that was just what my restless mind needed.

As though he could read my thoughts he told me that I was having a struggle with my own mind and that I needed to use the law of attraction to bring what I wanted into my life.

He reminded me that my negative thoughts were creating the negative things in my life and that I needed to start thinking positive thoughts if I wanted to turn things around. He said that despite that fact I was in love, I was feeling empty but not to worry because when I finally take control of my mind, my relationships will reach a higher level and happiness will soon by mine.

Unaware that I was on a two-month backpacking trip he added that travelling would give me strength. Then he offered to answer a yes/no question for me. Feeling completely embarrassed about asking this spiritually wise man such a silly question, I couldn't help but to spit out, "Will I ever be married?"

He had me pull a series of cards and after separating them into two piles of negative and positive cards he determined that the positive cards far outweighed the negative one signifying a possible yes. My heart smiled.

Despite the fact I have spent the majority of my life looking down on women whose only aspiration in life was to find a good man and get married here I was joining the club.

In fact, I was so scared of marriage that I used to have re-occurring nightmares about waking up married and trapped for the rest of my life. Why did I think marriage would rob me of my freedom?

He ended our session with a gift from Cuba – a picture of the Virgin Mary along with a recipe for controlling one's mind in affairs of the heart adding that happiness in relationships can only be achieved with a calm mind.

I returned to my hotel room with the recipe determined to whip up a batch of mind control but the recipe was in Spanish. D'oh…foiled again! The secret to finding a happy relationship continued to elude me.

As I processed this wisdom that had just imparted on me I realized it was nothing I hadn't already heard a thousand times before. The Universe has sent me countless books, lecturers, Facebook messages from God, audio tapes, dreams and fortune tellers all telling me the same thing. So why did I keep asking the same questions over and over?

What is it going to take for the truth to sink into my thick skull? Do I need to see it in skywriting? Does Elvis need to rise from the dead and sing it to me? Does God himself need to come down from the heavens and bitch slap me with it?

Lessons in Lost Luggage

My luggage finally arrived at 10pm on my last night in Bogotá. I had the choice of picking it up at the airport the following morning or having it delivered to the hotel. Out of fear it would get lost in transit, I told the Air Canada rep I would pick it up on my way to Lima. I figured I could survive one more night without it. Four days without luggage taught me a lot.

- I don't need as much shit as I thought.
- My depression and anxiety attacks will pass even without my medication.
- Clean underwear = happy camper.
- Everything will work out in the end whether I choose to have an anxiety attack over it or not.
- Hand soap does not make good shampoo.
- Gum can temporarily replace toothpaste and a toothbrush.

The next morning I arranged for a cab to take me to the airport three hours early giving me enough time to track down my luggage before checking it for my flight to Lima. My driver didn't show up on time so in a panic I ordered a new cab which cost me $10 less leaving me enough Columbian money to buy some souvenirs at the airport. After 30 minutes of frantically searching for the Air Canada office, I begged the lady at American Airlines to phone them and 15 minutes later a lady from Air Canada arrived with my suitcase. I wanted to hug it and do a happy dance around it but first I needed to find the check in counter for my flight.

As I boarded my flight I felt silly for feeling so anxious the past few days. In my heart I knew all along that everything would work out – it always does but that didn't stop me from running through every worst case scenario in my head until I was a nervous wreck.

Will I ever be one of those cool, calm and collected people? I sure hope so.

Life is about learning how to accept your own shade of crazy

– Teresa the Traveler

Top Ten Crazy Bogota Facts

1. Bogotá, the capital of Columbia, is the most populous city in the country, with an estimated 7,304,384 inhabitants as of 2009.
2. Guinea Pig racing is popular on the streets of Bogotá. A number of small plastic huts are placed on the ground and people place bets on which huts the guinea pigs will crawl into when the owner sends them off.
3. French fries are served with mayonnaise – one has to request ketchup
4. Instead of payphones there are people on the street that sell cell phone calls for $200 pesos a minute. The phones are chained to a stand.
5. Water is allowed through airport security and on the airplanes.
6. They are constructing a metro that is expected to be completed in 2015.
7. They celebrate Christmas well into January.
8. There are a number of different cabs; some are private with lump sum prices while others have meters. I found the metered ones to be cheaper in the city and the private ones better for long trips.
9. Columbia is combating its reputation as a dangerous country full of paramilitaries and coke dealers and is now promoting tourism.
10. It is not uncommon for meat to be grilling over an outdoor fire to be served in outdoor cafes.

▲ *Meat grilled on outdoor makeshift barbeques feed hungry pedestrians in street side cafes.*

▲ *Guinea Pig Racing is a popular form of gambling on the streets of Bogota.*

What Did Things Cost?

Items Purchased	Columbian Pesos	American Dollars
Hotel pick up from airport	$45,000	$25.00
Budget Hotel in Downtown Bogota	$73,000	$40.55
Public bathroom	$500	$0.25
Lunch	$20,000	$11.00
Round trip tram to Cerro de Monserrate	$8,000	$4.00
Cab from Bogota to Zipaquira and back	$170,000	$85.00
Entrance to Salt Cathedral in Zipaquira	$20,000	$11.00
Cup of freshly cut mangos	$1.000	$0.50
Tarot card reading	$10,000	$5.50
Cab to airport	$20,000	$11.00
Visa for Columbia	Free	Free

Lost in Lima

Happy to be reunited with my luggage, but even happier to be reunited with my happy pills I hopped the plane to Lima to meet up with my buddy Monique.

Oh yes…did I mention my friend Monique decided to join me for two weeks in Peru?

During the Christmas holidays, in an effort to calm my anxiety, I drove to Kelowna to hang out with my connections buddy Joel. I drove back to Kamloops via the Vernon highway passing through Monte Lake when I got the sudden urge to call my friend Monique…something I never do. She lived in Monte Creek and when she answered the phone I asked if I could drop in for coffee. I am not sure why but I never drop in on people. Lots of people including myself love it when their friends drop in out of the blue.

My fear of rejection usually stops me from doing this because I think they are going to be busy and not want to see me and if they do invite me in they are just being polite. How messed up is that?

Much to my surprise, Monique was home and delighted to have me drop in. Over coffee she confessed that she was having marital troubles – she and her husband had fallen out of love and were deciding whether to work on their problems or separate. She also mentioned that she needed to get out of town and go on vacation somewhere warm. Much like me, Monique gets restless and needs to go on a big adventure at least every two years to maintain her sanity. She was well overdue. Not one to procrastinate, when I invited her to join me in Peru she booked her flight that night.

▲ *The Palomino Islands are a sanctuary for sea lions and penguins.*

I drove home with a huge smile on my face and we spent the next few weeks excitedly planning our trip.

The Flying Dog

Monique had booked us rooms at the Flying Dog Hostel in Miraflores, the tourist area of Lima and that is where we started our big adventure together. Thankfully I had left my bulk of my blues in Bogotá and was ready for some serious fun.

I checked into my room and took a much needed shower before finally changing into some fresh clothes. Felling human again for the first time in almost a week, I joined Monique and a girl she had met at the hostel for an evening stroll around Miraflores.

Miraflores is an upscale district of Lima with flower-filled parks, great beaches for surfing and sun tanning as well as plenty of shops and restaurants. Established as a Spanish town in the 16th century, it was the scene of the Battle of Miraflores during the War of the Pacific where two thousand people died at the hands of Chilean invaders.

We walked through a cat-filled park then stopped for an economical dinner at one of the numerous Chinese food restaurants before heading back to the hostel and booking a tour of the Palomino Islands for the following day.

Developing World Connections

I emailed my friend Jeremy that night hoping to visit him and the Developing World Connections group at the jobsite but much to my dismay they had already finished the project and were preparing for the wrap up party. He and his group were in Peru to rebuild a condemned but important community centre so Peru's National Movement of Organized Working Children could use the building to meet, organize, learn and engage in social enterprise activities.

They spent the past two weeks moving rocks, mixing cement and painting. Their host-partner in Lima was IFEJANT, a Spanish acronym for 'The Training Institute for the Educators of Young, Adolescent and Children Workers'.

One of these days I would love to go on a project with this group. In case you haven't heard about them, here is an excerpt from their website developingworldconnections.org.

Developing World Connections are "a British Columbia registered society, Canadian Charitable Organization and a volunteer grassroots movement. We are non sectarian and have no religious, political or professional affiliations.

In the year 2000, President Wayne McRann and Director Dan Miller had been working on a Rotary project in the jungles of Guatemala assisting with the installation of a water system. The desire to share the joy of this experience spawned the idea of Developing World Connections. What began as an idea many years ago became a reality as the society was formed in 2004.

After the tragic Boxing Day tsunami, Developing World Connections quickly mobilized a grassroots response to help rebuild lives. We became registered as a charity in 2005 and what started as a grassroots response has now become a grassroots movement. Serving on four continents in twelve countries, *much work remains.*

Our multitude of volunteers, over 700 of which have participated internationally, have contributed hundreds of thousands of dollars and countless hours to worthy projects, volunteering abroad.

The tangible legacy of their efforts includes the rebuilding of an entire village in Sri Lanka devastated by the tsunami. Our volunteers continue to work on much needed infrastructure projects such as community centers, homes, schools and training facilities.

War of the Pacific

Taking place from 1879 through 1884, the War of the Pacific was a military conflict between Chile and the defensive alliance of Bolivia and Peru over the control of territory containing mineral-rich deposits.

The accumulation of vast amounts of high-quality nitrate deposits such as guano and saltpeter (key ingredients in explosives) in the Atacama Desert in Peru and Bolivia made the territory suddenly valuable. There was a high international demand for these minerals and Bolivia and Peru were sitting on the world's largest reserves.

The peace treaty that ended the conflict gave Chile the Peruvian territory of Tarapaca and left Bolivia as a landlocked country – a move that sparked Bolivian nationalists to long for the return of their coastline. In return, Chile agreed to build a railroad connecting the capital city of La Paz, Bolivia with the port of Arica, with Chile guaranteeing freedom of transit for Bolivian commerce through Chilean ports and territory.

Smells like Chilliwack

When we signed up for the trip the saleswoman promised we could swim with the sea lions making it sound as though we would be in a small boat. Dressed in our bathing suits, we felt a bit silly when our guide brought us to a huge 200-seat catamaran. This was not the tour we had signed up for.

Around an hour later we arrived at an island teeming with sea lions that swam playfully along the boat entertaining the crowd with their antics. I could not imagine swimming with thousands of sea lions and living to talk about it. Despite the fact it was quite a sight to see, the smell was overwhelming. When I asked Monique to describe it for our YouTube video, she said it smelled like a Chilliwack pig farm. I think she hit the nail on the head.

The next island had a large penguin population. I had no idea there were penguins in Peru. Who knew Peru would be where I saw my first penguin in its natural habitat. They didn't seem to do much aside from stand around having staring matches as though they were saying "What are you lookin' at? Are you lookin' at me? Why you lookin' at me?"

Creepy Catacombs

It was around 4pm by the time we got back from the tour and with some time still left in the day, Monique suggested we visit the catacombs. Catacombs'…isn't that where they bury people? Sounds creepy, let's go!

The San Francisco Monastery and Church were originally constructed in 1546, making it one of the oldest churches in South America. It also has one of the oldest and most historically significant libraries in the Americas with a dramatic collection of religious and secular art, including renaissance-era tiles imported from Spain. It served as the first official Catholic cemetery in Lima where, as per Roman custom, the dead were laid to rest in catacombs beneath the church. In fact if you look up into the grate from the catacombs, you can see the church.

We arrived just in time to join the next tour and, after checking out the library, cathedral and a number of other rooms in the monastery, we were brought downstairs to the creep catacombs. Our guide explained how the bodies were buried six deep in the first section and allowed to decompose before the bones were removed and buried again in one of the massive common graves. The catacombs were used until 1808 when the first cemetery was opened outside of Lima. Archaeologists excavated the site in 1943, and arranged the bones for public display.

Unfortunately people are not allowed to take pictures or video in the catacombs, but since I am a writer, I managed to get special permission and a private tour. Check out the video on my YouTube channel.

Watching Guards Change

After the catacombs we walked a couple of blocks over to the Plaza Mayor just in time to witness the changing of the guards at the Government Palace. Expecting something grand like the ceremony held at Buckingham Palace, we sat on the curb waiting for the procession.

An artist sat beside us with his portfolio and fought for our attention showing us each one of his masterpieces hoping to make a sale while we gave him an unenthusiastic "that's nice".

The entire ceremony took place behind the black iron gates of the palace and we could barely see it however, we continued to have a great view of some authentic Peruvian art.

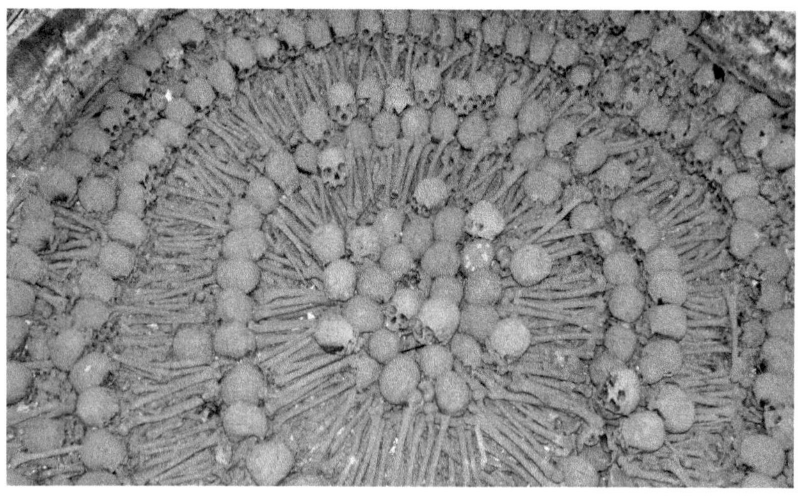

▲*Over 25,000 bodies have been buried in the catacombs beneath the San Francisco monastery and church*

▲ *The government palace has a violent history. It was built by Francisco Pizarro, the governor of New Castile and became his residence and government headquarters after the viceroyship of Peru was established. Pizarro and his mistress (the sister of the Inca Atahualpa he had strangled) were trapped by the Indians in the fortress in 1536 during a twelve day siege of Lim. In 1541, rebels broke into the palace and killed Pizarro who, although he was outnumbered, managed to kill two of them first. Pizarro's body was then buried in an unmarked grave in the Cathedral Church where it remained until 1977 when it was exhumed and put into the glass crypt in the church.*

I wanted to cross the street and get a closer look but the handsome policeman guarding the palace made sure that didn't happen.

When the ceremony was over we said goodbye to Mr. Artist and hoped he wouldn't follow us around the square. He didn't, instead every young school girl in Lima followed us around the square wanting us to pose for a picture with them. Why? I have no idea. Maybe they thought we were famous. Monique does resemble Cameron Diaz and I would like to think I look like Angelina Jolie....I said I would like to think...not that I do.

After a 30-minute photo shoot, we finally shook the tweens and explored the square which contained the Government Palace, the Cathedral of Lima, Archbishop's Palace of Lima and the Municipal Palace. Considered the historic center of the city, the plaza was mandated in 1523 by King Charles I of Spain.

In accordance with the procedures for the creation of cities in the New World, the main square was the first area to be established and the city grew along a grid centered on the square. Pizarro was quick to claim the large parcel of land between the north side of the plaza and the Rimac River.

The lot to the south was designated for the church, the western lot was to be the site of city council with the remainder of the lots divided amongst the rest of the conquistadors. The gallows was originally located in the center of the plaza but was later replaced with a water fountain.

San Martin Plaza

Having past by San Martin Plaza in the taxi on the way to the catacombs, we decided to walk back and take a closer look; however we had no clue how to get there. Asking for directions turned out to be more difficult than we had anticipated. I am so used to people around the world speaking English I was surprised how few people in South America spoke my native tongue. Having no clue what the name of the square was I resorted to a game of Pictionary with a jewellery store clerk hoping he could figure out where we wanted to go and give us directions.

I remembered the center of the square had a statue of a man on a horse so I drew a bad rendition of a stick man on a horse inside a square.

▲ *The fountain in the center of the square was once the location of the gallows.*

▲ *Construction of the Archbishop's Palace was completed in 1922.*

Twenty minutes into the game he still hadn't named that square and I was running out of new ways to draw it. Then suddenly Monique remembered that she had asked the taxi driver the name and wrote it down on a piece of paper and shoved it in her backpack. She pulled it out and announced San Martin Plaza and the clerk quickly drew us a map. The square was in exactly the opposite direction to where Monique and I had thought it was thus confirming neither one of us had any sense of direction. We were the blind leading the blind. Thankfully neither one of us was too attached to where we ended up. In no time we were admiring the plaza named after Peru's liberator Jose de San Martin, the Argentinean general and leader of the southern part of South America's struggle for independence from Spain. Inaugurated on July 27th 1921, in celebration of the 100th anniversary of the independence of Peru, the monument crowning the center depicts Jose San Martin emerging victorious during his voyage across the Andes.

After visiting the square and eating dinner at a chain restaurant called Norkey's (our new favourite eatery) Monique and I determined we had "done" Lima and it was time to move on and see the rest of Peru.

Top Ten Crazy Lima Facts

1. Construction on a huge ocean front promenade is in progress
2. Limans hate to stop at red lights to let pedestrians cross and often 2-3 cars will sneak through a crossing after the light is red.
3. The drivers in Lima love their horns and honk for pretty much any and every reason known to man.
4. Cuy chactado, or friend guinea pig, is a popular dish in the highlands. The indigenous women raise the critters in their huts where they run around loose and reach a surprisingly large size before they make their way to the dinner table.
5. The avocado comes from Peru and they produce the softest variety.
6. The weeping willow is origionally from Peru and produces the base ingredient for aspirin.
7. Maca, a Peruvian root, known as Huanarpo Macha is what VIAGRA is made from; it has been in use in Peru for hundreds of years.
8. The Amazon River starts in Peru. It is the largest river in the world by volume with a total flow greater than the next eight largest rivers combined).
9. Sunflowers, which are native to Peru, were domesticated around 1000 B.C. Francisco Pizarro found the Inca subjects using the sunflower as an image of their sun god. Gold images of sunflowers, as well as their seeds, were taken back to Europe in the early16th century.
10. The Plaza de Acho in Lima is the second oldest bull ring in the world. It was built in the days of viceroy Amat in 1766.

▲ *The colourful buildings in downtown Lima give the area a European feel*

▲ *The library at the San Francisco Monastery holds thousands of historical and antique books and documents.*

What Did Things Cost?

Items Purchased	Peru Soles	American Dollars
Palomino Island tour	218.00	$75.00
Single room in hostel	96.00	$33.00
San Francisco Monastery and Catacombs	7.00	$2.50
City tour on mini train	5.00	$1.70
Dinner (pork chops and salad)	20.00	$6.80
Taxi from Miraflores to downtown	13.00	$4.50
Silver necklace pendent	58.00	$20.00
Visa for Peru	Free	Free

Nifty Nasca Lines

While in Lima, Monique and I walked into a travel agency to get some ideas about where to visit next. When I saw a picture of this beautiful lagoon surrounded by sand dunes, I knew right away I had to see it. We discovered it was called an oasis called Huacachina located 5 km west of Ica. We booked a 5-hour bus trip to Ica where we took a short taxi ride to this truly unique paradise.

As we were waiting for the bus, Monique struck up a conversation with an American guy living in Peru and he recommended a great hostel. When she told him we were going to Machu Pichu, he also recommended we see a little known site similar to Machu Pichu called Kuelap. The trailhead to the site, which is still under excavation, can be reached by bus from Chachapoyas.

A two hour horseback ride or six hour hike will take you to the surprisingly unpopulated Inca site where you can see one of the most significant pre-Columbian ruins in South America.

Unfortunately the site was too far out of our way but we did check out his hostel recommendation and loved it. We got two rooms on the first floor surrounding the swimming pool in the courtyard.

I was surprised by how comfortable the bus was. My only Latin American bus experience to date had been years ago when my friend Carolyn and I backpacked through Central America. I remember riding brightly colored old school buses from one city to another once having to share a seat with an elderly Mayan woman, two kids and a goat.

▲ *Huacachina is a lagoon oasis located 5km west of Ica.*

▲ *The minute I spotted my first motor-taxi I knew I wanted to drive one.*

To make matters worse, the road was hot and dusty and the cabin was filled with cigarette smoke.

When we entered the non-smoking, air conditioned bus and walked up to the second level to relax in our spacious reclining seats, I was both relieved and delighted. To ensure our security, all the passengers were videotaped, the luggage was tagged and rules of the bus were played over a television set. The one rule I found a bit odd was regarding the on board bathroom. They requested that people only pee and if they require more, to inform the attendant who will have the bus driver stop either at a nearby washroom or the side of the road.

The safety video was followed by the Zac Efron flick *17 Again* which was followed by another: *Charlie St. Cloud.* In fact all the buses played Zac Efron movies making me wonder if it was law.

Adventures in Motor-Taxiing

On the way to Ica I noticed a number of these funky taxis that looked like a cart wrapped around a motorbike. I later found out they were appropriately called motor-taxi's. I loved them right away and had a burning desire to drive one. Yes, riding in one was not enough for me, I wanted to drive!

We booked a dune buggy tour which was not until 4:30pm (after the sand cooled down) giving us the day to explore Huacachina. When Monique and I stumbled upon a motor-taxi, we found the owner and convinced him to let us take it for a spin, which wasn't easy because he didn't speak a lick of English and our Spanish was nothing to write home about.

It was similar to riding a moped with one handle for acceleration and the other for a clutch and a brake on the floor. After a couple turns around the block we decided to let the owner take us around town at a break neck speed for a tour while we rode in the back hanging on for dear life.

With a few hours left before our dune buggy tour, we continued to explore Hauchachina by foot. Featured on the back of Peru's 50 Nuevo Sol note, this resort town built around a small natural lake in the desert is a popular getaway for local families from Ica and Lima. It is increasingly becoming a popular attraction for international tourists who come to surf on the hundred foot high sand dunes or blast over them in a sand dune buggy. Landowners living near the oasis have drilled wells which have lowered the water levels in the lagoon forcing the city to artificially pump water in to preserve its beauty.

The Shower Challenge

When I got back to my room to take a shower I wondered what sort of funky water issue I would face. I don't know what it is about South and Central America but you need a degree in plumbing to use their showers. Every shower seems to have its own unique way of functioning and I use the term "functioning" loosely. In Bogota I had exactly 2 minutes to enjoy warm water before it turned freezing cold. In Lima the shower gave me two minutes of scalding hot water before switching to freezing cold. Upon checking out two days later I discovered that there was a knob above the shower head that could be adjusted to warm thus making the hot water last a bit longer.

My shower started out fairly normal but after using up my 2 minutes of water I tried to turn the shower off but to no avail. I spun the knobs in both directions and water continued to flow. Then I saw a sign behind the toilet telling people to shut the taps off by turning them to the middle. It worked but still…WTF?

Sand Dune Surfer Girls

As we sat by the pool waiting for our tour operator to come grab us we met a couple from Chilliwack waiting for the same tour. How weird is that? We had spent the last few days joking about how the Palomino Islands smelled like Chilliwack and now we were about to go sand boarding with a couple from Chilliwack. This was the law of attraction in all of its glory but why of all things did we need to manifest that? Why couldn't we have spent our time focusing on getting paid to travel or perhaps winning the lottery?

Our guide Richardo finally came for us and packed us into his sand dune buggy – a large vehicle framed with steel tubing that accommodates approximately ten passengers. Never having been in a dune buggy, I had no idea what to expect. Thank God each seat was equipped with a *holy shit* bar because I spent the majority of the ride clinging to it screaming, "Holy shit"! Our driver kept the pedal to the medal as he flew up and down the sand dunes faster than a rollercoaster. More than once I got that zero-gravity feeling in the pit of my stomach. Once our adrenalin was flowing at maximum capacity, we stopped at the top of a large sand dune for some sand dune-boarding.

Much like snowboarding, dune-boarding utilizes similar equipment and requires a similar technique. Unlike the proper equipment that can be rented at shops throughout Hauchachina, ours were simple boards with Velcro bindings to fit over our running shoes - not very easy to stand up with. However they were great to lie down across and slide down the dudes at break-neck speeds and that is exactly what our group did. And by the end of our two-hour tour, there wasn't a crevice in my body that wasn't filled with sand.

When we got back to the hostel, I jumped in the shower and got ready for my shiatsu massage.

The Dirty Massage

I should have warned Monique but for some reason when I saw her in the lobby chatting with the receptionist and she asked me how my massage was, I answered "good".

We had booked shiatsu massages for ourselves earlier in the day thinking it would help us wind down after our sand dune tour. Mine was from 8-9 pm and hers was right after between 9-19 pm.

Expecting a female masseuse I was a bit surprised when a large Peruvian man introduced himself as the masseuse. I felt awkward and my gut told me to leave but I followed him anyway trying to tell myself he was a professional and everything would be okay. He led me to a private room with a massage table and instructed me to remove my clothes and he would be back in a few minutes. He also gave me a brief overview of what to expect and it sounded normal to me.

I stripped down to my underwear, which I always leave on during a massage. I figure there is nothing in that region that needs to be massaged by anyone other than my lover. When he came back in I was laying down on my front. He turned on some relaxation music and proceeded to massage my back and neck. The massage was pretty standard and I started to feel bad that I had judged this fellow based on his appearance. Just because he wasn't the standard petite Asian woman with strong hands that I was accustomed to, it didn't mean he wasn't just as capable.

My opinion quickly changed when he began to massage my thighs going as near to my crotch as possible without actually touching me there.

▲ *You haven't lived until you have boarded the sand dunes of Hauchachina.*

Not once but repeatedly until I became uncomfortable and started to tense up. As I lay there unable to voice my discomfort, I was reminded of Jacque, the massage therapist I lived with in Calgary.

In my late twenties, shortly after I got my interprovincial electrical certification, my friend Carolyn and I moved to Calgary to live with two girls, Shari and Liana whom we had befriended on a houseboat trip. Shari had rented a house and sublet one rooms out to a massage therapist named Jacque. Something about this man gave me the creeps. His room was next to where I slept, a sectioned off part of the basement with no door. One night I dreamt he was standing over my bed watching me sleep. When I told my friend Carolyn, she said she had the same dream. OMG – was this man creeping into our rooms at night?

One day I asked Shari about Jacque saying how he me feel uneasy. She then told me a story about how one of her friends had booked a massage with the guy and claimed he had molested her. That didn't surprise me one bit. Later that day I was talking to Jacque and asked him if he ever had the desire to have sex with his clients. He replied no but that sometimes when people are in such a state of relaxation they can imagine things. Past trauma can resurface making them believe it was done by the massage therapist. That logic seemed a little twisted for me so I made a point of avoiding this man until I could relocate to another house. I've been weary of male masseuses ever since.

When he asked me to turn over so he could massage my front I robotically did what I was told despite the fact he did not cover my chest with a sheet as is standard with most therapists. I tried to tell myself things are different in Peru than they are in

Canada and that naked massages are normal. He let a fair bit of time pass after I was flipped over before covering my breasts with a hand towel barely large enough to hide my nipples. As he massaged my stomach the towel fell off and when he made no effort to replace it, I did. He then attempted to push my underwear down and that is where I drew my line. I pulled him hand away telling him I did not need to be massaged any lower than my underwear line. I was wearing a low-rise g-string that just covered my hairline. What the...?

He backed off for a bit but when he massaged my thighs, he continued to move his hands farther up than appropriate forcing me to draw a line in my thigh and telling him to keep his hands below it. The massage ended with him running his hands lightly all over my body in a way that seemed more like the touch of a lover than one of a professional massage therapist. When the massage was over I jumped up eager to get dressed and out of there while he lingered in the room a bit too long telling me to relax, there was no rush.

Yes there was, I needed to get back to my hotel and shower this creepy man off me.

My head was cloudy when I saw Monique in the lobby awaiting her turn with the "Peruvian molesta-ssager". I wanted to warn her, I really did but for some strange reason when she asked me how it was I replied, "Good, I feel like spaghetti." Then I raced out and walked back to my room as my mind processed what had just happened.

An hour later Monique returned to the hostel and I was almost afraid to ask how her massage was. This was her first professional massage and she was not sure what to expect. Needless to say she found the whole experience rather uncomfortable. She was particularly disturbed by the kiss on the forehead at the end.

KISS??? My eyes grew as large as saucers and I shouted, "He kissed you?" She gasped when she realized she had just been taken. Although I think she was a bit relieved to know this was not what a professional massage was supposed to feel like.

▲ *Tourists flock to Hauchachina to take dune buggy tours of the surrounding sand dunes.*

▲ *El Candelabro is a large motif carved into the stone cliff near Paracas and thought by some to have served as a beacon for mariners.*

Just like me, her intuition told her something wasn't right but she ignored it believing this man to be a professional and thinking he must be following the standard procedure. I wonder if I will ever get over the guilt of not warning Monique that the guy was a creep. I was so excited about the prospect of getting a cheap one hour massage that I didn't think to ask questions. Lesson learned.

Actually I think the bigger lesson here is to listen to my intuition and never think that it is too late to back out of something. The guy was disgusting. Why on earth was I worried about offending him? If I had to do it all over again I would let him know exactly how I felt. Then I would pull a "Champ" on him. I would head-fake him with a bottle of massage oil, then give him so many lefts he'd be begging for a right. While I had him on the floor eating a tile sandwich I would look him in the eyes and say, "Is that enough kiss my buddy on the forehead for you?"- Ever since I've been Mrs. Champ.

Ballestas Islands

We woke up early the following morning and caught a taxi to Paracas for our tour of the Ballestas Islands. Composed mainly of rock covering an area of 0.12 square kilometers, these islands are a sanctuary for such marine species as the guanay bird, the blue-footed booby, the tendril, Humboldt penguins and a variety of seals and sea lions.

When we got to Paracas, Monique, me and everyone else in town, lined up at the pier to get onto one of the 30 person speed boats. After a brief stop at El Canelabro, we made our way to the spectacular Ballestas Islands – a bird paradise if I ever saw one. They even had a bird-crap collection agency located on the island that collects the poop for use as fertilizer. The area produces wine and the bird poop is used to fertilize the grapes.

The number of birds covering the rocky mounds and flying overhead was overwhelming. I was surprised that only one person from our entire boat got crapped on. Yes, it must have been my lucky day. I have had more than one bird take a dump on me in situations where it was the only bird and I was the only person in the area. Here I was in bird paradise and not one managed to hit my head. Either these birds are not as nasty as the ones in Kamloops or their aim is not as accurate.

▲ *A group of penguins engaged in starting contests on the Ballestas Islands.*

▲ *A mother sea lion and her cub bask in the sun.*

When the tour was over we returned to the hostel and hung out by the pool for a few hours before catching a two-hour bus to Nasca to try our luck at catching a last-minute Nasca lines flight. People had warned us to book our flight at least a few days in advance but Monique and I prefer to wing it so that is what we did. Our method had worked for us up to that point so we trusted our luck would not run out.

Nasca Lines

We arrived in Nasca with one goal in mind: to fly over the Nasca lines and the following day we did just that. A taxi picked us up and brought us to the Nasca airport, a small airstrip used almost exclusively to fly tourists over the Nasca Lines. Monique and I, along with three girls from the UK, piled into a small Cessna for a hurl-inducing 30-minute ride over the following formations: whale, triangle, trapezoids, astronaut, monkey, dog, condor, spider, hummingbird, Alcatraz, parrot, hands and tree.

Created by the Nazca culture between 400 and 650 AD, the hundreds of individual figures, made by removing the reddish pebbles and uncovering the whitish ground, range in complexity of design. Over 70 designs are of animals, birds, fish and humans while others are lines and geometric shapes. They were drawn in an area covering nearly 500 square kilometers with the largest figures spanning nearly 270 meters. The dry, windless climate of the Nasca Desert ensures that the lines remain well preserved.

The lines were discovered in the 1930's by people traveling over the area by plane and ever since, anthropologists have tried to uncover why they were made. They remain a mystery since flight had not been invented at the time they were constructed and the shapes can only be viewed from the air.

Archeologist Johan Reinhard published an article in 1985 theorizing that the lines were part of a religious practice of the Nasca people who worshipped mountains and other water sources critical to life in the desert. He felt the symbols representing animals and objects were meant to invoke the Gods' aid in supplying water and the lines were sacred paths leading to places were these deities could be worshipped. My theory is that they were created by parent to keep their children busy.

▲ *The Spider is one of the Nasca Lines.*

▲ *From top to bottom: Astronaut, Monkey, Spider, Hummingbird, Hands.*

From what I could see, the desert is pretty baron and there isn't much for kids to do. Their mothers probably sent them out during the day to turn over pebbles and stay of their hair until their household duties were finished.

Monique and I breathed a sigh of relief when we landed safely on the airstrip. Not only did we make it over the lines without hurling, we didn't crash either unlike the group of four Brits who along with their two pilots crashed in October of 2010 killing all six. In February of the same year, another plane crashed killing all seven on board. Poor safety standards were to blame for the incidents but the government stepped in and regulated the industry closing a number of the shadier companies down in the process.

Arriving in Arequipa

After the Nasca lines we hung out by the pool until it was time to hop the bus for the ten-hour ride to Aerquipa. This time we booked ourselves into first class which had larger seats that reclined all the way back.

We were sitting in the front row and had the best view of the latest Zac Efron flick – sweet! We didn't arrive at the Flying Dog Hostel until midnight and by this time we were both exhausted and happy to have a chill day to look forward to.

I loved the city right away, the cobblestone streets and colorful buildings had a European feel. Arequipa, the largest city in the Peruvian Andes, is the second biggest city in Peru, with a population of almost one million. Arequipa has more than 80 nearby volcanoes, most of which can be found in the Valley of the Volcanoes. Sitting at an altitude of 2,335 meters above sea level, Monique and I figured it would be a great place to acclimatize before heading to Machu Pichu. We had heard enough nightmare stories about people getting altitude sickness from riding the bus from Lima to Cusco and figured we would give ourselves some time to adjust to the altitude.

We headed straight for the main square where, after having countless menus shoved in our face from people on the streets who get commission for attracting people into the restaurants, we sat down for a tasteless breakfast. Afterwards we stopped in at one of the many travel agencies to check out what tours we could go on, most of which were two or three day trekking tours. There was no way I was going to get over my sinus cold by tenting in some canyon so it looked like I was going to get some rest whether I wanted it or not. We booked out plane tickets for Cusco for three days later and looked for creative ways to fill the time.

Wax on Wax off

Before I left on my trip, my friend Lexi waxed my armpits and I was hooked. I loved the feel of the smooth skin and was excited by the fact that when the hair grew back in it was thinner. No more shaving rash for me. A few weeks later I went for a legs and armpit wax at the local beauty school and I was good for the next month. By the time I hit Arequipa I was due for another wax and when I discovered a salon a few doors down from the hostel offering waxing for super cheap, I marched right in.

I questioned the salon's level of hygiene when I discovered pieces of wax melted onto the blanket covering the bed but I was so set on having my hair removed that I chose to ignore it. I signed up for armpits and lower legs and the lady started with my pits.

She coated both of them with a thick layer of wax and left it to cool. I found this odd because in Canada, the procedure is to apply the wax in one spot, place a strip on it, let it cool then quickly remove it grab a new strip and start again.

Once the wax had hardened she slowly peeled it off in one large piece allowing me to feel each individual hair being slowly removed from my armpit. OUCH! This was no spa it was a Peruvian torture chamber.

To make matters worse, once she removed the wax, she placed it back into the pot to re-melt…it complete with my hair. Horrified, I thought back to how they prepared the wax. I remembered seeing the lady plug the pot in, but I don't remember seeing her add fresh wax.

Yikes!

▲ *The locals love to hang out in the main square and feed the pigeons.*

How many other armpits had this wax touched? Would I contract some rare Peruvian armpit disease?

With the wax somewhat removed, she then started to pull out the remaining hairs with tweezers. In Canada this is a painless procedure as they are trained to pull fast and in the direction of the hair follicle. This woman was trained to do it slow in the opposite direction of the hair follicle making me yelp out loud and cancel the leg portion of the waxing.

When I got back to the hostel and told my Peruvian friend about my experience, he said the salon did it the old fashioned way but that there are many salons in Peru that do it the modern way. I think the lesson here is that it doesn't hurt to inquire first, a lesson I am slow to learn and wonder if I will ever. What is that saying…fools jump in where angels fear to tread?

Where the Bleep is Waldo?

Being an avid mountain biker and member of the Kamloops Bike Riding Association, Monique was eager to do some mountain biking in Peru. So when we walked past a tour company offering bike trips down the side of a volcano, she couldn't resist.

We were fully aware of the fact that Puruvian salespeople had a tendency to tell you whatever they thought you wanted to hear in order to close the sale but we still believed the guy when he said we would get mountain bikes with full suspension, all the gear including elbow and knee pads along with a box lunch. He also said the tour went from 9am until 4pm; all for $65 – much more than the other companies charge for the same tour as we later discovered.

Two men in a Range Rover with bikes on the roof picked us up at our hostel and drove us up the rocky winding road for 2.5 hours until we reached 4,800 meters up Nevado Chachani - the highest mountain near the city of Arequipa.

As a result of the very low precipitation in the area, Chachani, a popular mountain for climbers, does not have a permanent ice cap or glaciers. Many tour agencies in Arequipa offer guided trips to the 6,075 meter summit, though the altitude is considered highly challenging for those who are not fully acclimatized. Base camp is at approximately 5,200 meters with another higher camp called Camp Azulfrera situated at about 5,400 meters. The standard route requires crampons and an ice axe, but does not require roping up, as there are no large crevasses on Chachani and the average total climb time from base camp ranges from six to nine hours, with a two to four hour descent.

From Chachani, we got a fantastic view of El Misti – a stratovolcano also known as Guagua-Putina. Near the inner crater six Inca mummies and rare Inca artifacts were found in 1998 during a month-long excavation. These findings are currently stored at the *Museo de Santuarios Andinos* in Arequipa.

▲ *Monique and I wait while the guides fix my bike yet again.*

▲ *There is an insane number of taxicabs filling the streets of Arequipa.*

When we arrived at the drop off, we quickly realized that the tour did not in fact come with full riding gear, a box lunch or even proper bikes. No, that's not true…our guide had a lunch, full safety gear and a bike with full suspension, while our bikes didn't even have proper braking systems. Mine were standard brakes which I quickly discovered didn't work. As for safety equipment we were given ill-fitting helmets and gloves.

Once we were on our bikes and ready to go, our guide shot off like a bullet and we spent the next hour playing "Where's Waldo." The sandy side trails and rocky main road were not easy to navigate and to make matters worse, the brakes on my bike were locked on and my gears would not change

Monique and the guide were way ahead of me and once we got to a hill I had to get off my bike and walk. When the truck caught up to me I got in and we caught up to the guide. By this time I was PMS'ed off. Yes, I got my period that day and my bullshit tolerance was at a record low. I asked the guide where the hell he picked up my crappy bike…the dollar store or was it homemade.

I then went on to tell him that for the price we paid, he should ride the crappy bike and I should ride his bike.

Monique could sense my anger and before I bitch-slapped our guide and the two of us ended up abandoned on the side of a volcano, she offered to let me ride her bike. I jumped at the opportunity figuring since I was the slow one, Monique and the guide would easily catch once they fixed my bike. Unfortunately that did not happen. I stopped on the shoulder for 15 minutes and they were nowhere in sight. Then I looked across the valley and saw the truck taking a different route down. What the…?

I noticed that the road met up with mine near the bottom of the volcano so I quickly peddled down to meet them. The guide had made the executive decision to have Monique peddle his bike on the pavement behind the truck while they took a short cut to catch up to me.

How insane is that? Monique could have rode the same path as me and caught up to me much quicker. The driver and guide then drove off and told us to meet them at the next town leaving Monique and I to ride for 30 minutes through garbage dumps and slums in order to catch up to them…not fun. By the time we reached them I was ready to go postal. To make matters even worse they stopped at the bike rental place to return the bikes before delivering us to our hostel. I can't believe this tour company did not even own mountain bikes. They just rented cheap ones for the day. Lesson learned – if you mountain bike in Peru, rent your own!

Fantasy Island

By my last day in Arequipa it finally hit me that Antonio would not be emailing me. Perhaps he would call the next time he came to Kamloops but that wasn't enough. I wanted more. I wanted the full meal deal and Antonio either could not or would not give it to me. It didn't matter which it was they both hurt. I felt like such a fool for wanting it in the first place. I don't know what hurts me more, the end of the relationship or the end of my fantasy around what could have been. Most likely it was the latter. The fantasy was way better than the reality and I knew it.

The relationship had brought me much more pain than pleasure. Antonio was emotionally unavailable and despite the fact things were great for the first few months, they had been going downhill faster than a brakeless car ever since.

I was seriously starting to wonder if there was such thing as a passionate relationship that didn't end in heartache. I have certainly never witnessed one in my 41 years on the planet. But I couldn't give up hope because that was all I had. That was what made me get up every morning and face the world. The hope that one day I would be in a secure loving relationship.

The one thing I have come to realize during my time on Earth is that love truly is the spice of life – without it everything is just okay. I didn't want okay. I wanted great.

But first I had to get through the next few weeks. My body was filled with sorrow that could only be released through tears. I made sure to stuff my backpack full of tissues because I would need them.

▲ *Monique enjoys a magnificent view of Arequipa's town square over breakfast.*

Top Ten
Crazy Peru Facts

1. The deepest canyons in the world are located near the city of Arequipa. The Cotahuasi is 3600 meters and the Colca is 3400 meters deep.
2. There are usually charges of $1-$5 dollars on top of tour prices. Such things as airport tax, sand tax and park taxes are charged.
3. The police rarely pull people over for speeding and if they do $5 US will usually get you out of the ticket.
4. It cost less than $100 US a month to rent a one-bedroom apartment in Ica.
5. The planes that fly over the Nasca lines usually only fly in the morning when the winds are calm.
6. In many of the budget places you are not allowed to flush toilet paper down the toilet, you must throw it in the garbage.
7. Peruvians like to serve French fries with everything in fact they even put them in stir fries – I call this dish the stir French fry.
8. There seems to be an area to cater to every need, for instance, all the computer stores are in one area, there is a street full of guitar stores, a bookstore street, the stores around the main square all sell tours and a number of streets are dedicated to cafes and restaurants.
9. Many of the local women wear their hair in two long braids under a straw hat.
10. Pisco, a colorless grape brandy developed by Spanish settlers in the 16th century, is the local drink of choice.

▲ *All over Arequipa were local ladies on the street making and selling little dolls.*

▲ *Really cool, reasonably priced jewelry is sold all over the streets of Peru*

What Did Things Cost?

Items Purchased	Peru Soles	American Dollars
Single room in hostel	60.00	$20.00
Sand dune buggy and sand boarding tour	45.00	$15.50
Bus from Lima to Ica	58.00	$20.00
2.5 liter bottle of water	3.00	$1.00
Taxi from Ica to Huacachina	6.00	$2.00
Dinner (chicken and rice or spaghetti)	10.00	$3.40
One hour Shiatsu massage	25.00	$8.60
Tour of Paracas Reserve	75.00	$25.80
Bus from Ica to Nasca	35.00	$12.00
Single room in Nasca	85.00	$29.00
Chinese dinner for two	11.00	$4.00
Flight over Nasca Lines	290.00	$100.00
Silver bracelet with Nasca designs	100.00	$35.00
Silver men's ring with Nasca designs	40.00	$14.00
Airport tax	20.00	$7.00
Chair massage 15 minutes	20.00	$7.00
Bus from Nasca to Arequipa in first class	120.00	$45.00
Armpit wax	20.00	$7.40
Single room in hostel in Arequipa	75.00	$27.00
Bag of groceries (fresh fruit, chips, juices, yogurt)	25.00	$9.20
Mountain bike tour down the side of a volcano	175.50	$65.00

On the Road

Hotel Business Card

Make sure you have purchased travel medical insurance before you leave. Not every country has free universal medical and if you end up in a hospital it could cost you an arm and both legs. Insurance can be purchased online and through most banks and insurance companies.

Tourist Information Booths

There are a number of recommended and required shots and medications one needs to get before traveling to South America and they are not cheap. A full set could cost over $300. Be sure to get them at least a few weeks before you leave as you could experience cold and flu symptoms after getting them.

Negotiating a Taxi

Negotiating a taxi when you first hit a new town or country can be a harrowing experience that will often end up with you getting hosed if you aren't careful. Here are some tips to keep you on the dry side of said hose. Ask a non-taxi driver how much the fair should be. Compare fares with other drivers and barter your way to a good price. Be willing to walk away and if he lets you that was the price and you will know for when the next driver approaches you.

Time Zones

When you reach a new city always ask a local what time it is. You may be in a new time zone and not even know it. If you are not careful this could cause you to miss tours, trains, buses and planes.

I am embarrassed to admit it, but I know this from experience.

Town Square

It you are a person who likes peace and quiet, you may not want to rent a room that overlooks the town square because on the weekends and in the evenings, there is usually some loud activity taking place involving dancing and singing.

Toilet Paper

Make sure to always carry some tissues or toilet paper in your day pack because many of the public washrooms do not supply this luxury. And remember to throw it in the garbage – do not flush it down the toilet as the septic systems in South America can't handle it.

Exchanging Money

Do not exchange money at the airport unless you absolutely have to because they offer the worst exchange rates ever. I usually take out local currency from a bank machine on my credit card once I am in each country. While you do have to pay a fee for each withdrawal you also get a fair exchange rate. A good way to find out the rate before entering the country is to look online. Google exchange rate and find a rate calculator. Also be aware of certain shady exchange places that will slip in a few bills of different worthless currency to trick you. My friend from Ireland changed some Argentinean pesos into Bolivian and the clerk slipped in a 1000 Chilean pesos instead of 1000 Bolivian – a huge hit to his travel budget.

Picchu Party Train

Having watched all the Zac Efron movies we could possibly stomach, Monique and I decided to fly from Arequipa to Cuzco rather than take the bus. We arrived first thing in the morning and after finding a cozy hostel to hang our hats for the next five days, we went about booking some tours. The Sacred Valley tour, a day of visiting some minor Inca ruins was the most common day tour unfortunately the two things that interested us most, Moray and the Inca Salt Pans were not included.

They were a different tour so we booked that instead thinking that next to Machu Picchu who cares about the other Inca ruins?

Moray

We met up with our tour group the following day at 9:30 and boarded a mini bus for Moray – an archaeological site approximately 50 km northwest of Cuzco on a 3500m high plateau.

The site, consisting mainly of several enormous terraced circular depressions, the largest of which is about 30 m deep, was possibly used by the Incas as an agricultural experimentation center. The depth and orientation of these depressions with respect to wind and sun creates a temperature difference of as much as 15 °C between the top and bottom.

This large temperature difference may have been used by the Inca to study the effects of different climatic conditions on crops. It also boasts a sophisticated irrigation system as do many Inca sites.

I sound like an expert on the site but when we were there, Monique and I ditched our tour guide and wandered around the site on our own. Figuring it must be some sort of religious site we made our way into the center of the bottom circle and put in our requests to the Inca gods. Monique asked for clarity and I, of course, asked for love.

▲ *Archeologists believe Moray to be a site where the Inc conducted agricultural*

▲ *The individual salt pans are privately owned and handed down from generation to generation.*

Not that I didn't trust the Universe to deliver, I just figured a little help from the Inca gods couldn't hurt.

I laughed at the irony of our situation. What Monique wished for most was the ability to travel around the world. Her trip was coming to an end and she was not ready to return to her husband and kids. What I wanted most in the world was the husband and kids. In fact, part of the reason I travel the world is in hopes of meeting my true love.

I wondered if the two of us were just caught in the rut of wanting what we don't have. If we got what we wanted would we both be happy or would we just long for the next thing we thought we couldn't live without?

Inca Salt Pans

Our next stop was at Salineras de Mara or the Inca Salt Pans. Located fifty-eight kilometres from Cuzco in an isolated part of the valley, it consists of thousands of mismatched white squares plotted along a steep green to brown hillside with a small salty creek coming out from the mountain. The small plots are filled with water and upon evaporation a crystallization process takes place and salt can be panned out. Used for centuries, the salt pans were allotted to the citizens of Maras with each one getting a certain number of the plots to which they keep the profits of the salt that is packaged and sold. Families pass the plots down from generation to generation like heirlooms. On any given day workers can be seen doing the exhausting, back-aching extraction process.

Not interested in the lecture, Monique and I quickly left the group to explore on our own and marvel at the small salty stream that trickled into the salt pans. As we snapped pictures of each other we came across a Frenchman named Charlie who was on a two-month motor bike adventure throughout Peru. He reminded me of my friend Kevin who I was supposed to tour with in Columbia.

Charlie and I quickly discovered we shared a passion for photography and engaged in a conversation about cameras. He was handsome with a boyish face and patchy sideburns and I felt a tiny crush forming as the two of us connected. Unfortunately I had to return to my bus so I regrettably said goodbye thinking who knew I would meet a guy in the salt pans in Peru. I think the Universe was reminding me that I could meet the man of my dreams anywhere.

Town Crier

Later that night Monique and I walked around the main square searching for a place to eat dinner when we heard some loud music and cheering and went to investigate. It was Saturday night and some entertainers had visited the square to perform for the crowd. A full band complete with a horn and percussion section played traditional music while dancers dressed in traditional Peruvian costumes performed traditional dances.

The crowd was energized and a feeling of celebration filled the air. Unfortunately that feeling evaded my airspace. I wanted to have fun but my eyes kept welling up with tears so, instead I sat on a park bench trying unsuccessfully to contain myself.

Why did I have to keep mulling over why things weren't working out between Antonio and I?

I wanted so badly to just let it go but didn't know how. An older woman with an eerie resemblance to Antonio's mother caught my eye. I liked his mom as much as I disliked his dad and because of this I was drawn to her Spanish doppelganger.

The woman saw me staring and gave me a warm smile. Tears started to flow down my face. Much to my surprise she ran over and embraced me consoling me in Spanish. I don't usually cry in public as sadness is an emotion I try to keep to myself but I couldn't help it. There I was in the middle of Cuzco crying into the arms of a complete stranger and it felt good…much better than crying alone and much better than pretending to be happy when I'm not.

Maybe the Universe was telling me that I don't have to get through this alone. Perhaps the only way I could get through it was with the help of others.

Machu Picchu

Built by the Incas in the 15th century, Machu Picchu was used as both a religious shrine and a palace for the Inca emperor. Located midway between the tops of two mountains 450 meters above the valley and 2,438 meters above sea level, the main area of the site contains 172 buildings. However, the extent of the ruins covers an area of 32,592 hectares throughout the Vilcanota-Urubamba river basin in what is called the Sacred Valley.

Some people choose to reach Machu Picchu by way of the Inca Trail – a three day hike starting at kilometre 82 of the train route to Cuzco, but Monique and I aren't those people. We chose to stay dry and ride the train. They don't call it the rainy season for nothing and the idea of camping in the rain for three entire days did not appeal to either of us. We are backpackers not sponges.

A taxi picked us up at our hotel at 6:30 am and, because the train tracks between there and Cuzco were being repaired, brought us to a charter bus for a two hour drive to Ollantaytambo – try saying that five times in a row while spinning in a circle. From there we boarded a two-hour slow, and I mean SLOW, train to Aguas Calientes where we caught a 20-minute bus ride to Machu Picchu. It was after 11:00 am by the time we got there but we didn't have to catch the bus back down until 5:30 pm giving us plenty of time to explore.

We started our journey on the upper trails eager to capture that perfect "I was at Machu Picchu" picture. After about 50 takes, we got hungry and went to chow down at the buffet. Our timing could not have been better because moments after we sat down, it started to rain…then pour…then downpour. They say it rains a lot in the Andes but I had no idea it rained this much. We sat out the storm for about 3 hours before returning to check out the village.

I must admit I did very little research about the site before visiting. I think I was afraid that if I anticipated it too much I would be disappointed – after all, expectations do have a tendency to decrease joy. It must have worked because I had no idea what to expect and Machu Picchu far exceeded any expectations I did have. I could see why in 2007, following a vote of 100 million voters worldwide, Machu Picchu was declared one of the new wonders of the world along with Chichen Itza, the Roman Coliseum, Christ Redeemer, the Great Wall of China, the Taj Mahal and Petra.

We wondered through the narrow cobblestone paths that wound their way through the stone houses then circled the site to view it from every possible angle.

As we approached the exit I stopped. Not quite ready to leave I went back to have my own Machu Picchu moment while Monique waited near the gate. I found a private spot near an ancient Inca house and admired the magnificence that is Machu Picchu.

My heart burst with joy when I thought back to three months prior when I bought a cork board and pinned places I would like to see on it. On it was a picture of the scene I was witnessing. I had no idea my wish would come true so fast. My eyes welled up with tears and I thanked the Universe for this amazing opportunity.

For many visiting a site like Machu Picchu would seem like the impossible dream. For me, finding my forever man seemed like the impossible dream. It occurred to me that I needed to relax and trust the Universe. I put it out there that I want to meet him and I needed to trust that the Universe was guiding him to me.

The Universe has made all my dreams come true thus far so why wouldn't it give me the one thing my heart desired most?

I took a deep breath and watched the mist descend from the mountains and make the village disappear. Then when I least expected it the mist would rise and the ruins would reappear like a freshly unwrapped Christmas present. My heart filled with joy and gratitude for the gifts the Universe had given me and would continue to give me.

▲ *The mist over Machu Picchu comes and goes all day covering the village then disappearing.*

Party Train

When we got to the train station we ran into two guys from the Czech Republic that we had met on the upper viewing area. One of them had been kind enough to take a picture of Monique and me. His friend was really hot so I insisted he pose with us. I just can't resist tall handsome men and John was one of those men. The divorced furniture importer was on a one-month Peruvian adventure with his friend Mark, a Czech military airplane mechanic.

With 40 minutes to wait until we boarded, I had plenty of time to sit with the guys and get to know them better. Or should I say sit with John and get to know him better. The chemistry between us was so intense that the rest of the world seemed to momentarily disappear. I was disappointed to discover we were in separate cars thinking I would probably never see him again. I figured his was only another walk on role in my adventure designed to remind me that I had options: Antonio was not the only stallion in the stable.

Monique and I sat across from a Chilean man and his young daughter and while Monique and the girl played games with a Canadian penny, I listened to dance music on my MP3 player. Feeling an incredible high from my amazing day, I was too full of energy to sleep so instead I imagined a dance party breaking out on the train and me busting a few moves.

My fantasy was interrupted when the train made a sudden stop and we were informed that there was a rock on the track, which later turned into a few rocks and ultimately translated into a landslide caused by the torrential rains. The tracks were covered and it was uncertain how long it would take workers to clear them. Our day was already long after leaving our hotel at 6:30 am with an estimated return time of 11:00 pm. Who knew how long it would take us to get back to Cuzco? Deciding there was nothing I could do I resigned myself to my seat and settled back into my dance party fantasy until I noticed some of the people from our car looking into the car in front of us. I got up to join them and saw a group of people congregated in the aisles of the next car. Thinking perhaps they were able to see the landslide, I grabbed my camera and went in hoping to get some pictures.

I bumped into John and Mark sitting near the door so I sat down and chatted with them. I quickly discovered that the crowd was a group of Frenchmen drinking at the bar and listening to music. They seemed to be having a good time and I was about to join them when the attendant from my car came over and made me return to my seat.

I sulked back into my car where I watched through the window and witnessed the party picking up momentum. People were starting to dance. What the…? That was my dance party. How dare this woman prevent me from joining it! Suddenly John peeked through the window and motioned for me to come back. I wanted to, I really did but I was afraid of getting kicked out again. Damn fear of rejection…why did it have to rear its ugly face now? I knew we were going to be there for quite some time – landslides don't clear themselves and I would rather be joining the party than watching it from my seat. So I served my fear of rejection a tall glass of shut the hell up. With Monique covering my back, so the attendant could not see my escape, I marched over to the next car grabbed John by the hand and brought him to the bar and asked him to buy me a beer.

The next five hours were the most fun I've had in years. John and I drank Pisco shooters with a group of egg farmers from Montpelier, France and the party was on. We discovered an I-pod dock in the train's stereo system and when one of the passengers offered up an I-pod full of dance music, the dance party in my head suddenly became a reality. I started to bust a move and so did everyone else. No pun intended, the group formed a train and chugged through the middle of the aisle picking up any strays. Then we did the Macarena and the YMCA and any other moves we could conjure up.

When the music slowed down, John invited me to slow dance. Snuggled tightly into his chest I could not resist my urge to kiss him. Not usually one to make such a bold move, the combination of high altitude, Pisco and the desire for any man's lips but Antonio's to be the last to touch mine made me lose all control. Much to my surprise, John resisted my advance telling me it was too soon.

What the…? In my estimation our relationship started five hours prior and would expire in approximately four more. I felt it was the perfect time for a kiss but at the same time I admired his modesty. It made me want him even more.

The final song of the evening was one of my favorites, *I've Got a Feeling* by the Black Eyed Peas. As I sang along "I've got a feeling that tonight's going to be a good night", I thought back to my weekend at the connections retreat. At the end of the second day the DJ had played that same song and the entire group got up and danced. I wanted to join them but I didn't. I couldn't. I had forgotten how to have fun and was not able to force myself to get up and dance.

It never occurred to me until that night how guilty I had felt for going to Afghanistan, and getting paid to have fun while people all around me were getting killed. I needed to let myself off the hook and acknowledge that the war wasn't my fault and there was nothing I could have done to stop it…but how? That was why I went to South America in the first place: to remember how to have fun. And there I was – letting loose on a makeshift dance floor on a train in the middle of the Andes with a bunch of people I had just met. I didn't have a care in the world and it felt great.

After five hours, the track was finally cleared and the attendant successfully ushered me back to my seat for the remainder of the ride.

When we disembarked in Ollantaytambo, John was waiting to say goodbye. I handed him my card and told me to find me on Facebook. He said he did not have an account but would start one just so we could keep in touch. Sure I thought…just like Antonio promised. Not going to hold my breath for that one. I wanted to believe him, I really did but my heart was guarded. I guess only time would tell if he was a man of his word.

As we wondered around the chaotic scene looking for our bus amongst the mess of buses and taxis John drove past in his rental car and stopped for a final goodbye. He rolled down the window and I ducked my head in. He kissed me goodbye then drove off into the night. The next morning he contacted me on Facebook and the day after that I flew to Buenos Aires while he drove to Puno to visit Lake Titicaca making me wonder if our paths would ever cross again.

Top Ten Crazy Sacred Valley Facts

1. A lot of young travelers and hippy kids from around the world hang their hats in Cuzco for a few days, months or years. Some even earn money on the streets selling jewellery or braiding hair.
2. People wanting to take the four-day hike up the Inca trail to Machu Picchu often book months in advance.
3. During the rainy season you can expect rain almost every day – if you forget to bring a rain jacket or umbrella, they are readily available from vendors at the front gate.
4. Those wanting to hike the trail to the very top of Machu Picchu must get there early in the morning and line up as there are limited passes issued at the gate each morning. Many backpackers walk up to the entrance from Aguas Calientes to beat the people taking the first bus.
5. There are a lot of local women on the street selling handmade Peruvian dolls; so many that I finally had to buy one.
6. It is hard to walk past a restaurant without someone shoving a menu in your face and trying to usher you inside. I think these people get a commission but all they did was scare me off.
7. Inca walls line both sides of the alley along Loreto as you leave the Plasa De Armes (Cuzco's main plaza). On the left is the oldest Inca wall in Cuzso.
8. The vicuna is the national animal of Peru and is used in the Peruvian coat of arms. Once an endangered species, they now thrive although are still at risk from poachers and loss of habitat.
9. The Sacred Valley was one of the empire's main points for the extraction of natural wealth, and one of the most important areas for corn production in Peru.
10. In colonial documents the Sacred Valley is referred to as the "Valley of Yucay".

▲ *Handmade Peruvian dolls are readily available everywhere in Peru.*

▲ *When I pinned a picture of Machu Picchu to my dream board, I never imagined I would be visiting there three months later.*

What Did Things Cost?

Items Purchased	Peru Soles	American Dollars
Single room in hostel	74.00	$26.00
Flight from Arequipa to Cuzco	475.00	$176.00
Inca Salt Pan and Moray Tour	50.00	$18.00
Machu Picchu (transportation and admission)	518.00	$185.00
Chicken dinner at nice restaurant	20.00	$7.00
Buffet at Machu Picchu	92.00	$33.00
Handmade Peruvian doll	15.00	$5.00
Train dance party	Priceless	Priceless

Don't Cry You're in Argentina

My first night in Buenos Aires did not go quite as I had anticipated. Rather than spend all night doing the Tango with a sexy mysterious hunk of a man, I sat in my room feeling lonely and depressed.

I missed my travel buddy Monique who had a way of cheering me up. After a good cry I wiped my tears and forced my sorry butt out the door to check out this vibrant city.

Buenos Aires is the most beautiful city in South America with the most beautiful people. Even the homeless men sleeping on park benches could be cleaned up and put on the cover of GQ.

Located on the west bank of Rio de la Plata, this city of 3 million is part of a larger conglomerate called Gran Buenos Aires which has almost 13 million people making it one of the largest urban centers in the world.

Evita Museum

While wondering the streets, I came across a sign pointing to the Evita Museum and knew right away I had to visit. I have been a fan of Evita ever since watching Madonna in the musical film about this politician/actresses amazing life. In 1944, at age 24, actress Eva Duarte met widower Jaun Domingo Peron at a ceremony held at Luna Park where she was honoured for raising funds for the victims of an earthquake that devastated the city of San Juan. In the seven short years her husband ruled Argentina, Evita improved the lives of the poor and the workers through legislation and construction. Children received education through Home Schools, the Children's City, University Cities and the One Thousand Schools Plan and a safety net was created giving all citizens access to health care.

▲ *Greater Buenos Aires is one of the largest cities in the world.*

▲ *Evita was considered by the masses to be the spiritual leader of Argentina.*

The Eva Peron foundation constructed hospitals, nursing homes, schools, summer camps and provided scholarships to students and housing subsidies. The foundation also held mass at the end of each year where they provided cider and sweet breads to the poorer families.

Eva was also instrumental in fighting for women's rights such as equality in marriage and parental rights and helping to achieve women's suffrage. Unfortunately the woman, who many referred to as the spiritual leader of Argentina, had her life cut short due to cervical cancer and that is when the craziness began.

After her death on July 26th 1952, the government declared a 30-day national mourning. Her procession, which passed through the streets of Buenos Aires, was followed by over two million people while others threw flowers from nearby balconies. Her body, which was embalmed, was then put on display for two years while her final tomb, a statue larger than the Statue of Liberty, was being constructed. However, on September 23rd 1955, after Peron's government was overthrown by the Liberating Revolution forces, her body was kidnapped and hidden for 16 years. The military finally revealed the location of her corpse; she had been buried in a crypt in Milan Italy under the name Maria Maggi.

In 1971 her body was exhumed and flown to Spain where it was kept on the dining room table in the home of Juan Peron and his third wife Isabel Peron who, upon the death of her husband, was elected the first female president in the Western Hemisphere. Isabel returned Evita's body to Argentina and after briefly displaying it beside the body of Juan Peron, had it buried in the Duarte family tomb in Buenos Aires' Recoleta Cemetery.

Father Tango

After the museum I did some shopping on the large pedestrian street and noticed a number of people carrying signs offering tango classes and shows. Considering this sexy dance began in the working-class port neighbourhoods of Buenos Aires, I figured I ought to check it out.

A bus picked me up at my hotel at 7pm and drove me to the tango club where I was led into a room lined with chairs. I had signed up for a tango lesson before dinner and wondered who I would end up doing the tango with. The room filled up with way more women than men making me think I may be partnered up with another woman…not how I imagined learning to tango but oh well.

The sexy spanglish speaking instructor had a few tricks up his sleeve to accommodate such situations. First we walked in a circle learning how to step to the beat then we were separated into men and women and taught some moves. The men were then instructed to ask a woman to dance and every few minutes had to switch and dance with a different woman giving us all the chance to practice with a man letting everyone get to know each other.

After our lesson we were seated at a table in a dinner theatre room where we ate a three-course meal before being entertained with a tango show. The performance was incredible and the meal was edible…yes, just edible but the show more than made up for it.

I was seated with a young couple from Germany and a retired 76-year-old Catholic priest from the United States.

Unfortunately the tango lesson, as fun as it was, wasn't enough to wipe the pout off my face and I was so anxious about having to make small talk with these people that I almost got up and moved to another table to be by myself.

I do believe everything happens for a reason and if I was seated with these people then I was meant to get to know them and that's what I forced myself to do. When the priest asked what brought me to Argentina I told him I was traveling around South America looking for love. He replied, "So you are looking for your soul mate." After 41 years of never having been in a relationship that lasted longer than a year, I had some serious doubts about the idea of a soul mate. I cheekily said you mean sole mate…the man I date exclusively.

The father then defined the difference between a sole mate and a soul mate. A sole mate teaches you how to love someone while a soul mate teaches you how to love everyone. Wow, that was deep. I spent the rest of the evening contemplating that thought. Was there really someone out there who could inspire me to love everyone? I would sure like that because as it stood, I found most people annoying and could not imagine loving them all. How could I love everyone when I could barely love myself?

Sensing my uneasiness and inability to feel comfortable in my own skin, the father said that since I was kind enough to share my story with the table, he proposed each of them offer me a gift of what they wished I would find on my journey. The German girl said she would like for me to love myself so that I can let go of my need to find love because once we detach from what we want that is when we receive it. Her boyfriend wished for me to find a place where I can be still for awhile and heal while the father wished for me to see myself the way others see me: as a loving, adventurous and beautiful woman. My eyes welled up with tears as I accepted their love. I could feel my depression starting to lift and thanked the Universe for sending me help in my time of need.

As we parted ways the father gave me a little more food for thought regarding my feelings of failure for still being single at 41. He said it was better to spend 10 years with the right partner than a lifetime with the wrong one.

Isn't it Ironic?

Upon arriving in Argentina, I was flipping through my Lonely Planet guide to see what there was to do when I came across a write up on Iguazu Falls. They wrote, *"People who doubt that negative ions generated by waterfalls make people happier might have to reconsider after visiting Iguazu Falls. Moods just seem to improve the closer you get, until eventually people degenerate into giggling, shrieking messes."*

That sounded like my kind of place so when I came across an office for Argentina Airlines, I stopped in and bought a plane ticket to Puerto Iguazu. As I stepped off the plane I was greeted with a blast of warm humid air. The heat was so intense I thought I was going to melt. I asked at the airport information desk where I could find a budget hotel and the receptionist recommended I look near the bus station so I had a taxi drop me off there.

First I tried the hostel across the street from the bus station but they were full so I tried a number of other nearby hotels and none offered single rooms and if they did, they we full. This was harder than I thought. Tired of dragging my luggage around from place to place, I asked a friendly hotel clerk if I could leave my luggage with him while I looked.

His hotel only offered double rooms and he did not speak English so I was not able to determine if I got the room to myself or if he reserved the option of giving me a roommate should one come along.

I walked around in the heat for another 30 minutes getting nowhere until I was exhausted and ready to take a chance on the double room. He led me to a dark room in the corner of the hotel where I deposited my luggage and changed into my swimsuit for a dip in the pool. From the pool I could see some rooms on the second floor with a view that looked more suitable so I inquired.

Apparently they were single rooms but they did not have air-conditioning and because of that they were cheaper. I was willing to forfeit air-conditioning so I changed rooms.

I lugged my luggage up the stairs, unpacked then took a shower. I had come to realize that just because a place said they had hot water it didn't mean they did. However what I really wanted was a cold shower so I didn't care. I turned on the tap fully expecting to cool down and out came a blast of hot water that lasted the entire duration of my shower. I tried to cool it down but to no avail, the shower had one tap that came in one temperature: hot.

I had finally lost my attachment to having a warm shower so the Universe decided to reward me with one...great timing Universe. If I could just detach from finding a man perhaps I be rewarded with one of those too. I am sure if Alanis Morissette was on hand she would be singing *isn't it ironic.*

I later realized that that the water tanks in Iguazu were located on the roofs in order to take advantage of solar energy. The temperature of the showers was directing related to the temperature outside. Nice.

▲ *My room was the middle room on the second floor.*

▲ *Iguazu Falls is easily one of the natural wonders of the world.*

Iguazu Falls Happy Dance

First thing the following morning I took the city bus to Iguazu National Park to chase some waterfalls.

Located on the boarder of Brazil and Argentina, the falls divide the river into the upper and lower Iguazu. Consisting of 275 falls along a stretch of 2.7 kilometres, two thirds of the falls are within Argentine territory. The majority of the individual falls are about 64 meters in height with some reaching up to 82 meters high. The most impressive fall is the U-shaped Devil's Throat at 82 meters high, 150 meters wide and 700 meters long.

I had booked the grand tour from a travel agent in the city but if I could do it all over again I would simply buy my tour directly from the booth at the park. I had to go there anyway to redeem my voucher and had I lost it, I would be hooped. Unbeknownst to me, I could have bought just the boating under the falls part of the tour for much cheaper but instead I got the full meal deal.

It started with a short jeep tour through the jungle where we saw one spider and a bunch of trees, then we went on a boat ride up the river where I saw no spiders but plenty of trees and then we arrived at the falls where we took one pass for pictures, then stowed our cameras in the waterproof bags provided and drove right up to the falls for a very wet close up. The entire trip cost about $56 while the last part, which was the most fun, cost only $25. Oh well, live and learn.

At least I was kind enough to warn some other tourists, the backpacker's equivalent to flashing your lights to alert other speeders of a cop. You've got to look out for each other.

After getting good and soaked from the boat ride, which was quite refreshing with the extreme heat, I spent the rest of the day on the catwalk; yeah on the catwalk I watched the waterfalls from the catwalk. *Gotta like one hit wonders like Right Said Fred.*

I was absolutely blown away by the beauty of the falls and completely amazed that I had never heard of them– did I live under a rock? I thought Niagara Falls in Canada was amazing but this place made Niagara look like tap water. By 4 pm I was burned to a crisp and exhausted so when I discovered I could return to the falls the following day for half the price, I did just that. I arrived at the park when it opened at 8 am and was first in line at the ticket office. I was determined to spend some time alone at the base of the falls so I could film myself doing a happy dance.

Yes, you read that right…I performed an Iguazu Falls happy dance. Inspired by *Where the Hell is Matt* of YouTube fame, I decided to do a little bad dancing of my own at my favorite sites. My first dance took place at Machu Picchu and by the time I reached Iguazu Falls I couldn't wait to perfect my moves. Thankfully I was able to beat the crowds and find a place to perform without a huge audience. I have some pretty funky moves and I didn't want anyone to steal them…but mostly I didn't want to explain to a plethora of tourists what the heck I was doing.

While standing at the foot of the falls performing such moves as the sprinkler, stirring the pot, the Macarena, the spank, staying alive and running on the spot, an older couple from the United States witnessed my crazy antics.

Determined to get the footage I needed for my music video, I continued to dance as though I was displaying completely normal behavior. When I was done, I stuffed my camera into my backpack, wished the couple a good day then went on my merry little way.

Water Falling

Later that night I came across an advertisement for a tour that included repelling down a waterfall. I marched into the tour office and signed up. Yes of course the idea of repelling down a waterfall scared the living crap out of me. I am not a *complete* idiot. But that was exactly why I booked it. I firmly believe that in order to feel truly alive you must do at least one thing every day that scares the crap out of you. I came to South America to feel alive again and this looked like a great way to achieve that.

Having already zip-lined in Maui (on a much grander line), the zipping portion of the tour was little more than a relaxing ride over the jungle. It wasn't until the waterfall portion of the tour that my adrenalin started to pump.

▲ *At the bottom of the waterfall was a warm pool where we all went for a dip.*

▲ *Repelling down a waterfall is more fun than I could have imagined.*

I looked over the edge and could not imagine stepping out on that platform and walking down the front of the waterfall. Giggling like a little school girl, I immaturely taunted the others about repelling down fully aware that I was not the only one shaking in my boots.

When it was my turn I was determined to descend the entire falls without slipping. Some of the others had slipped and it didn't look fun. Heart pounding, I carefully chose each foothold reminding myself to breath and stay calm. Slow and steady wins the race. One exhilarating step at a time I descended the waterfall while another girl on the tour stood at the bottom with my camera and recorded the entire event. When I reached the bottom without slipping, I was so proud of myself. I Teresa the traveler repelled down a waterfall. Yeah me!

I love overcoming my fears. It gives me confidence and makes me stronger. My mantra was one I got from motivational speaker Tony Robbins, "everyday in every way I am getting stronger."

World's Worst Birthday Card

My friend Cindy had celebrated her 45th birthday and emailed me the card her boyfriend of 3-years had sent her from Germany where he was living for the winter. It read:

Dear Cindy Happy Birthday.
Another year gone by and I would like to thank you for being there for me when I was down. I know I'm never really there for you and never really will be, I think you knew that when we met but as long as we can still have fun together and meet it is still ok. We don't owe each other anything. I hope you understand. Unfortunately I built my life here years ago...
You look better than ever.
All the best love Chris.

I have no doubt she would have preferred a card that read: I am sorry for being such a jerk and failing to contact you for weeks on end while I was away. I have realized I love you and promise to make it up to you. Thank you so much for your patience and for supporting me even when I didn't deserve it. Your true love forever and ever…Chris.

My heart ached for Cindy as the card may as well have been addressed to me from Antonio. I had come to realize that he was happy with the situation as it was but I wasn't. I wanted more. There had to be something better out there and I was going to find it. But how?

Sometime when you quit trying to solve a problem, the Universe steps in and solves it for you — Teresa the Traveler

Be the Party

I hate it when I wake up in the morning with that pit in my stomach and that feeling of hopelessness and despair. Unable to drag my butt out of bed and convince myself it will be a good day, I usually spend the day on the couch longing to go back to bed where at least I can have happy dreams. I had woken up feeling that way enough in the past year…I was done.

Much to my surprise, despite the fact I had no big plans for the day, I woke up on my last day in Iquazu feeling peaceful and content. I decided to just hang out and have a much needed chill day and avoid the sun as I was already burned to a crisp. The Universe was kind enough to turn down the heat and send in some rain while I relaxed in my room and edited pictures and video of the past few days.

Filming and editing my Iguazu Falls happy dance had done wonders for my well being. It reminded me to be the party. I had spent the past four years trying to be a part of someone else's party and forgot what it was like to be my own. No shit I always felt like I was on the outside looking in and feeling constantly out of place.

I remember many a time in my 20's when I felt out of place wanting to be anywhere or anyone else. If I was sitting in a pub with a friend and saw a large group having fun, I would wish I were partying with them. If I saw a beautiful woman kissing her boyfriend, I would wish I was her. This all changed one night on a house-boating trip with my friends.

Every May long weekend, some girlfriends and I rented a houseboat and cruised around Shuswap Lake looking for parties and men. There was a group of guys from Calgary that we befriended and often parked beside at beach parties. One year they brought a friend along and sparks flew between us. We spent the first two nights hanging out and having a great time but something shifted on the third night.

The guys were having a party on their boat and all of us girls were there and the object of my affection was paying attention to everyone but me leaving feeling a bit insecure. As I felt my mojo escape my body and crawl around on the floor, I started to wish I was anyone or any place else.

Determined not to spend my last night on the boat feeling like a loser, I listened to the little voice in the back of my head when it told me to go back to my houseboat and find my guitar. I walked back to my boat, grabbed my old Gibson, and marched up to the top deck to strum out some of my favourite Johnny Cash songs.

Although I was all alone, I no longer felt lonely, instead I felt happy and at peace with myself. I was totally in the moment forgetting all about "what's his name".

Nothing eases stress like singing Folsom Prison Blues and within no time my mojo decided to come back. At that moment I heard a voice in the dark announce "I found her" and six guys from another boat came over to join me. They had seen me from six boats away and came over for a sing-a-long. Soon other people overheard the singing and joined us and before I knew it, my guitar and I were the life of the party. By the time my friends returned the party was in full swing and I had completely forgotten what was troubling me.

I need to do that more often when I am feeling out of place…be the party. Take a deep breath, bring myself into the moment and remind myself that I am where it's at.

Later in the afternoon I went online and read Kevin's latest blog entry to see if he was any closer to making it to South America. He had been stuck in Panama for the past few weeks waiting for bike parts – the drawback of using your own mode of transportation. I loved reading his blog because he has a unique way of putting into words everything that flows through his mind. I found his honesty quite refreshing. He wrote something quite profound that festered in my head:

I have been thinking about coming home for the summer. I have to be sick of it. And as of late I am not quite there yet. I have told a lot of people that I am coming. It wouldn't be the first time I have disappointed. People just don't get it. I hang with them and get on with them but when it comes down to it I am always alone in my own dingy adrift in the sea of life. I suppose that everyone is in their own dingy. I have yet to meet another backpacker who gets it. Perhaps Teresa does. I get a tingling that she does but I have yet to travel with her.

Did I get it? I used to but I had forgotten. I was so afraid of drifting in my own dingy that I had been seeking refuge in everyone else's then being disappointed when they didn't bring me where I wanted to go. It was high time I re-inflated my own dingy and trusted my own navigational skills. Thanks for the reminder Kevin.

Thoughts from the Asylum

Wondering where to go next I closed my eyes and flipped through my Lonely Planet Guide and let the Universe decide. I stopped on pages 216 and 217: Uyani Bolivia, home of Salar De Uyuni, the world's largest salt flat – an endless tableau of mind-altering vistas and wild rock formations. That sounded interesting so I did some research and learned that flying to Salta was step one.

When I arrived at the Salta airport the first thing I had to do was pee and apparently so did every other woman on the flight. I ended up third in line, not good. One thing I hate about being a woman is waiting for the ladies room. Granted it is usually cleaner than the men's bathroom but it can take forever to get in. What on earth do women do in there for 15-20 minutes? Do they have sponge baths, pluck their nose hairs and give themselves a perm? I rarely ever spend more than 3 minutes in there. Even the worst case of traveler's diarrhoea could only extend that by a few minutes.

▲ *Iguazu National Park is filled with every color of butterfly imaginable and they are everywhere often landing on visitors.*

The universe doesn't always give you what you want when you want it, but it always gives you what you need when you need it the most - Teresa the traveler

As I stood there impatiently doing the "I have to pee dance" and wishing the ladies ahead of me would hurry the bleep up, I looked longingly towards the men's bathroom that of course had no line up. At that moment I wished I was a man. Aside from the bathroom issue I am quite happy being a woman. In fact when I work on large construction sites where there are hardly any women I usually get my own washroom trailer. At those times I am really happy to be a woman.

Thankfully an airport worker pointed out a larger woman's bathroom and a bunch of us walked over to use it. I briskly passed the other women ensuring I got into a stall first. I felt completely justified in doing so because I only took a minute and who knows how long each of them would take.

After I retrieved my luggage I walked outside the terminal where the taxis were lined up. I always hate taking a taxi from the airport to town because they often try to hose me. Most tourists have no idea how much it is supposed to cost and the drivers totally use this to their advantage. Sometimes I ask a few different taxis what the price is hoping to get a better deal and that often cuts the price by a few bucks. This time I got lucky and the price was cheap so I didn't look around. The cabs in Salta were metered so there was no need to negotiate.

I missed Monique because she liked to research towns before we got there and always found us great hostels before we even reached town.

I can't be bothered and usually show up with no clue as to where I am staying. Usually I get the taxi driver to drop me off near the bus station or the main square because both locations are good hunting grounds for budget hotels.

It's not like North America where accommodations are best found on sites like Hotels.com, Expedia or Travelocity. The best deals in South America are often found by referrals from other travelers, guidebooks or from walking around the main areas of town.

A map in my guidebook told me that Plaza 9 de Julio was the main square so I had the driver drop me off there. He stopped right in front of the Colonial Hotel, which looked like the type of place I usually went for. The rooms had views of the square and the common areas were clean, spacious and quiet. There was a sign at the reception desk with the room prices posted but I disregarded it knowing there is always room for negotiation when you show up off the street.

▲ *This was the view of Plaza 9 de Julio from my room.*

▲ *One of Salta's beautiful old churches*

A room rented out at a lower price is always better than an empty one. They knocked $20 a night off when I told them I wanted the room for three nights.

Oddly enough that hotel was also recommended in my guidebook – a fact I noticed as I was sitting on my bed flipping through it while watching the drama unfold in Cairo's Tahrir Square.

The week-long protest calling for President Mubarak to resign was beginning to get violent with rocks and Molotov cocktails filling the skies above the square. Some of the protestors were members of the Muslim Brotherhood, an organization that had been accused of using terrorism as a means of imposing starker Muslim law on the country making it more like Saudi Arabia and Iran.

Five years ago when I was in Cairo the brotherhood were holding protests on the street and waving banners on the side of the road as my taxi drove me to my hotel. That was the first I had ever heard of them. My Egyptian friend Joe was afraid of what would happen to the country should they gain power.

While Mubarak's supporters also hit the streets, those calling for his resignation claimed they wanted democratic freedoms not allowed under his regime. There was concern over who would step in to take his place if he were to resign before the next election. Foreigners were being encouraged to leave the country and diplomats were running for cover.

The rumble in my tummy sent me onto the street in search of a meal. I went on my usual recognizance tour of the neighbourhood looking for the necessary amenities: bank machine, drugstore, fruit stand, and restaurant with English menu and/or pictures of menu items, travel agency with English speaking clerk and most important: ice cream stand. As luck would have it I found all six with two blocks of my hotel making me one happy backpacker.

After lunch I booked a tour of the salt flats then returned to my room to peel the skin off my back. When am I going to get smart and start using sunscreen? I had some in my backpack.

My peel-a-thon was interrupted by two small birds tweeting on my windowsill. I quickly closed the window so they wouldn't fly into my room and forget how to get out. Birds can be so dumb. I had a feeling they would be my Salta pets. In every place I go I always seem to have a pet of some sort. Sometimes it's a dog or cat, in Iguazu it was a gecko who hung out on the wall by my door and in Belize it was a monkey named Nancy. Nancy was male. I have no idea why they gave him a girl's name.

Around 5 pm I set out again to take some pictures of the city while the sun was setting. I came across a beautiful red and white church and snapped a few pictures but didn't bother going in. Catholic churches

depress the hell out of me. The walls are usually plastered with pictures depicting the Stations of the Cross with a huge statue and/or picture of Jesus hanging from the cross somewhere near the pulpit.

Don't get me wrong, I do believe a man named Jesus walked the earth and preached the word of God but why do we insist on reliving his death over and over. What a gruesome and painful way to die.

Jesus did so much good during his short time on the planet so why can't we focus on that? Why can't the churches decorate their walls with pictures of him performing miracles, healing the sick and preaching to word of God? Thinking about that makes me want to go to church – images of a naked man nailed to a cross wearing a thorny crown doesn't…just saying.

I must have stepped over 3 sleeping dogs on my way back to the main square. Sleeping dogs are everywhere in South America, they seem to be installed on every street corner and store front. You don't see dogs sleeping on the streets in Canada. They sleep on living room floors or on the edges of beds. When out on the street they are usually going for a walk with their owners, working security or leading the blind. We don't tolerate lazy-ass dogs.

I was in the mood for Italian so I stopped by a café near my hotel where I had already eaten twice. Their food was crappy but I keep returning. Why…because at least I am familiar with their crappy food – the same reason I keep eating at McDonalds.

At least their food was better than the place I ate the day before. I ordered a ham and cheese sandwich which came with barely a trace of ham. What kind of precision instrument did they use to cut the ham so fine? Rest assured few pigs are sacrificed each year in the making of these sandwiches. I guess that's a good thing if you're a pig.

Of course they did not have an English menu, most places didn't. In Italian restaurants if doesn't really matter because spaghetti, pizza and lasagne are the same in every language. However I was also craving salad, something I rarely crave, which could explain that extra 20 pounds I continued to pack around. Ordering salad was not as easy since none of the Spanish words for vegetables even remotely resembled there English counterparts. I pointed to what appeared to be a mixed salad and hoped for the best.

As I waited for my spaghetti and mystery salad it occurred to me that I should have brought a Spanish/English dictionary to help me in those situations. No…that would make too much sense.

A bowl of lettuce and tomatoes arrived at the table which in my definition is not a salad. A salad must contain at least three different ingredients. How could they call this a mixed salad? It was a bowl of lettuce and tomatoes. A woman dropped off a small bowl of grated cheese along with some oil and balsamic vinegar which I added to the lettuce and tomatoes thus forming what I considered a reasonable salad.

Next was the spaghetti…a bowl of plain spaghetti noodles. What the…? Who the heck taught these people how to cook Italian? Would some Italians please immigrate to Argentina and open up a decent restaurant?

After another disappointing meal, I hit the square, which was virtually empty during the day with the majority of the shops closed but came alive at night. Wall to wall people jammed the streets to walk, socialize, shop and watch the street performers. I am not a fan of large faceless crowds. I find them lonely and annoying.

People on the street are always trying to sell me something, beg for money or give me a cheesy pick up line. Some of the men absolutely disgust me with their hisses, whistles and desperate looks. I am clearly not interested in you so why do continue to be creepy? Do you honestly think it will make me reconsider?

Sometimes I put on my sunglasses and MP3 player and tune them out which makes some of them quite upset. What's up with that? It's my attention and I will give it to you when and if I want! Not all the people on the street bother me. Some just leave me alone or smile and say hi…I like those people.

It wasn't long before I retreated to my hotel room, closed the window and put in my ear plugs, which didn't help. I could still hear the thumping of music from the street performers.

These people really love loud music. If it is not turned up to the point of distortion they are not happy. It was quiet when I booked the room I had no idea it would be so noisy at night. Noise never really bothered me until I hit my mid-thirties. It used to be the case that I loved noise and wasn't happy unless there was a television or music playing in the background. Now my favourite sound is silence. I wanted to march out onto the street, unplug their amps and send everyone to bed so I could get some sleep. OMG, am I one of those people...a cranky old woman at 42?

Of Mud and Men

Fourteen hours is way too long to be on a tour. The guide picked me up at 7 am in a Ford Explorer then we drove to another hotel to pick up three young women from Buenos Aires. We had barely left town when the engine started to skip. The last thing I wanted was to be stuck in the middle of the desert. It wasn't long before the temperature gage was at hot and we had to pull over in a small village.

▲ *Our guide drove us through a cactus filled canyon on the way to the salt flats.*

▲ *When I posted this picture on Facebook, my friend commented that it was the biggest prick she had ever seen.*

I am not sure how it happens but I have witnessed this strange phenomenon throughout the world. For some reason, moments after an engine breaks down and the hood is opened it is surrounded by men. There could be no men in sight and the broken engine will make them magically appear out of nowhere.

Within minutes of the breakdown there is usually up to six men bent over the engine displaying a horrific case of mechanics crack. Most of the men know nothing about engines but can't resist the urge to join the others around the hood to discuss the problem. The one who produces the wrench is usually the one with just enough knowledge of engines to be dangerous. He will inevitably start loosening and tightening things while having the driver turn the engine on and off.

During this engine party, the women usually stay in the car or go for a walk to get as far away from the vehicle as possible in case it blows up.

The day was not off to a great start. My prognosis of the situation was a crack in the radiator. It was a ridiculously hot day and we were driving through a desert…not a great combination. After 30 minutes they managed to cool the engine down and fill the radiator with enough water to keep the engine cool for another 20 minutes before it once again overheated.

Having experienced this problem with my truck a few years back, I suggested to our guide that he turn on the heat which would cool the engine. Heat in a car is just hot air sucked from the engine and brought into the cab. This in effect cools off the engine. My guide didn't believe me and we spent the next few hours stopping on the side of the road at regular intervals while he continued the arduous process of adding water to the radiator even burning his hand in the process.

Knowing how guys love to fix things, I sat back and let him do his thing until it became apparent that we would never make it to the salt flats at that rate. I was going to do a happy dance on that salt flat if it killed me so I took matters into my own hands.

The next time the engine heated up I turned on the heat full blast and insisted he trust me. He laughed when it did not go down immediately then after a minute the gage moved towards cool and stayed in the middle – a safe place to drive. He was shocked and grateful for this new information.

Considering we were out of water in the middle of the desert we didn't have many other options…well there was water from the mud puddles formed alongside the dirt road from the heavy rains of the past few days. He had resorted to using it once and how he managed to fill the bucket up and pour it into the radiator without getting his clean white shirt dirty was a mystery to me.

Unfortunately our problems didn't end there. We were on a dirt road that had recently become a mud road. A large truck was already stuck forcing us to negotiate the best way around the bad patch. Our guide had befriended the driver of another tour van and the two were excited to face the challenge together.

What is it with men and mud? I swear the first thing a guy does when he gets his driver's license is find the biggest mud bog he can get his truck stuck in. This way he and his friends can spend the next few hours testing their strength by pushing it out thus giving them reason to celebrate with a man party. That is exactly what happened, the van got stuck in the mud and they spent the next thirty minutes pushing it out and then the man party chewed up another 15 minutes.

I was getting a bit grumpy by this time. We were already 8 hours into the tour and had seen nothing of interest aside from a few large cactuses, a greasy spoon café and an old train.

I couldn't believe we stopped to see a train. People keep old trains in their backyards in Canada…they are not that exciting.

It wasn't until around 5 pm when we finally reached the salt flats which I must admit were pretty cool. It looked like a moonscape so I incorporated a moonwalk into my happy dance.

Salinas Grandes is a salt desert covering an area of 8,290 km^2. The area is of industrial importance because of the sodium and potassium that are mined there. Perhaps one day Lithium will be too. While these salt flats are the largest in Argentina, they paled in comparison to the Salar de Uyuni in neighbouring Bolivia.

Disappointed that we didn't get to spend much time at the salt flats, I was glad to start the four hour drive back to Salta. I didn't get to my room until 9 pm which made for a long day…too long. Despite the fact much of the day was spent doing my least favourite activity: waiting, I must admit I admired our guide's attitude. I would have turned around the minute the truck started acting up and called the whole thing off. In fact, I never would have braved the roads had I known I might get stuck in the mud. Despite the fact things always work out in the end it doesn't stop me from worrying about them.

▲ *A young couple goes for a stroll along the salt flats.*

▲ *Salta has a tram that brings people on top of a hill overlooking the city with beautiful gardens and waterfalls.*

I loved that our guide trusted we would complete our tour and even when things looked bad he kept a positive attitude taking things one step at a time. I need to do that more in life…quit worrying about everything and just take things one step at a time.

Fortunately the day ended on a happy note. I checked my email when I got back and received a nice letter from John saying he hoped I was thinking about him and that he had a week left in Peru before he returned home. It made my heart smile. I also got an email from Cindy saying that she finally talked to her boyfriend and cleared up the issue of the world's worst birthday card. What he was trying to say was that he felt bad leaving for 6 months of the year and wouldn't blame her if she wanted to end it and date someone else. He knew she was sad and lonely when he was gone. That being said, he admitted he loved her very much and still wanted to be with her. I was happy things worked out for them.

Why Settle?

On my last night in Salta, I was determined to eat a proper meal. The usual bowl of lettuce and tomatoes that I had been settling for did not satisfy my craving for vegetables, it just pissed it off. Certainly there was a kitchen somewhere in this city that knew how to make a proper salad. I walked into one place and glanced over their menu. When I saw some of the items written in English I thought I had hit the jackpot. It made no sense to me that the restaurants did not provide English menus to cater to all the tourists. At least the brochures and maps were in English…that's a start. Unfortunately, after I sat down, I realized only the drinks were in English.

What the…? Did their English-speaking customers not like to eat? I requested an English menu from the waiter and when he couldn't provide one, I contemplated settling for whatever I could get. Then I though why settle? I settle too much in my life. How am I ever going to get what I really want if I continue to settle With that thought I marched out and went back onto the street looking for what I really wanted: a good meal. The next place I found did not have an English menu but it had an English-speaking waiter which turned out to be even better. When he asked me what I wanted I said a chicken salad with an assortment of vegetables. Apparently that was not on the menu but could be ordered from the kitchen. When he brought back a bowl of chicken salad with lettuce, tomatoes, mushrooms, celery, onions, cheese and even a walnut, I wanted to sing halleluiah.

After my salad-success, I had the confidence to take care of a few other needs. I wanted gelato and I wanted to buy it from a place where I could just point to the flavour I wanted and the type of cone I wanted. Most of the ice cream stores kept their ice cream hidden in the freezer in metal containers with the flavours listed in Spanish on a board above. The first place I walked into wasn't sufficient so I continued my quest and much to my delight, the second place was exactly what I wanted. Grinning ear to ear, I pointed to the café gelato and a sugar cone. That was easy. In fact it was so easy that I decided to tackle the issue of cold medication. The children's chewable tablets that I bought in Buenos Aires were doing nothing to ease the sinus congestion I was battling. I prefer to buy my medications in English for obvious reasons. In Syria I bought what I thought was Imodium. It made my diarrhoea even worse. Perhaps the Arabic speaking pharmacist thought I mean constipation instead of diarrhoea.

A short walk down a street leading off from the square brought me to a large pharmacy with shelves full of medications. They even had recognizable brand names which is not common in most South American hole-in-the-wall pharmacies. When I saw a package of Benadryl for cold and allergies I got excited. B-bye runny nose!

After getting what I wanted I felt good. No…I felt great. I loved that I didn't settle. Holding out for what I really wanted took a bit more time and effort but it was well worth it in the end. I need to do that in all areas of my life..

I lost count of how many times I settled in relationships and never got what I really wanted. Let that be a lesson to me. I determined then and there that Teresa the traveler does not settle!

▲ *A series of walkways called the Garganta del Diablo lead visitors out to the top of Union Falls.*

Top Ten Crazy Argentina Facts

1. They don't charge for a visa to get into Argentina but they do charge what they call a reciprocal fee to citizens of all countries that charge them for visas equal to the amount that it costs an Argentinean citizen to visit that country.
2. The residents of Buenos Aires love to jog, it must help them to look as fabulous as they do.
3. When a man on the street walks past a woman he finds attractive he will sometimes make kissing noises. While I found it creepy it was nice to know I still had it going on.
4. Many of the shops in Iguazu close in the middle of the day for nap time, except the leather coat shops. Why? I have no idea. It was so hot in Iguazu that I felt like I was going to melt making me wonder who the heck was buying these warm jackets.
5. I believe it is nearly, if not completely impossible, to find a decent meal in Iguaza, I made several attempts but to no avail.
6. Many of the businesses in Iguazu do not have air-conditioning including the restaurants and many don't even have fans making you simply drip with sweat when you walk in.
7. Many Argentineans like to chew on coca leaves which are believed to treat gastrointestinal ailments, motion sickness, act as an anti-depressant and help with weight loss.
8. It is illegal to bring coca leaves or any coca products into the US and Canada because the illegal drug cocaine is derived from coca.
9. Yerba mate, a popular drink in Argentina, is prepared by steeping dry yerba mate leaves in warm water and drinking it from a shared hollow gourd with a metal straw.
10. The mansion that houses the Evita Museum was purchased by Evita's Foundation in 1948 and transformed into a shelter for women and children.

▲ *Boat tours bring visitor right up to the falls where they get soaked.*

What Did Things Cost? 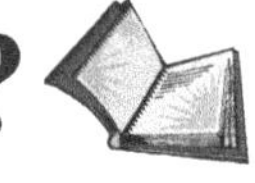

Items Purchased	Argentina Pesos	American Dollars
Single room in downtown Buenos Aires	206.00	$53.00
Flight from Cuscoa to Buenos Aires	2184.00	$560.00
Visa for Argentina	292.50	$75.00
Taxi from airport to Buenos Aires	120.00	$30.00
Tango class, dinner and show	300.00	$77.00
Evita Museum	15.00	$3.80
Bus tour of city	70.00	$18.00
Flight from Buenos Aires to Iguazu	755.00	$193.00
Taxi from airport to bus station in Iguazu	80.00	$20.00
Single room near bus station in Iguazu	150.00	$38.00
Lunch	30.00	$7.60
Boat and Jungle tour of Iguazu Falls	220.00	$56.00
Waterfall repelling and zipline tour	150.00	$38.00
Bus to Iguazu Falls	15.00	$3.80
Entrance to Iguazu Falls	100.00	$25.00
Boat Tour of Iguazu Falls	100.00	$25.00
Flight from Iguazu to Salta	1267.00	$325.00
Taxi from airport to Julio Square in Salta	25.00	$6.00
Single room in Julio Square in Salta	200.00	$50.00
Salinas Grandes Tour	250.00	$64.00
Crappy ham and cheese sandwich	10.00	$2.50
Tram ride in Salta	15.00	$3.80

Raining and Chile

Crossing a boarder on a bus sucks. Buses usually carry around 50 plus passengers and when you reach the boarder, that's how many people get processed alongside you. Needless to say, the odds of one of them having an issue with their passport are quite high. Of course that's what happened on the bus from Salta to San Pedro. When we reached the boarder we stopped to get exit stamps from Argentina and one of the ladies ran into an issue that held us up for four hours while the authorities attempted to solve it. I had boarded the bus at 7 am expecting to arrive in San Pedro by 4 pm giving me plenty of time to find a hotel. That did not happen.

Wrestling with Mud

We did not arrive in San Pedro until 8 pm and after spending an additional hour at the immigration office getting our passports stamped and having our luggage checked by security it was nine before I started my search for a room. From what I had heard, San Pedro was a popular tourist town with plenty of tours available which is why I was so surprised to be parked on a dirt road. Actually it was a mud road thanks to the heavy rains they had been experiencing.

At first I thought that this was just the outskirts of town and once we cleared customs we would get back on the bus and get dropped off at the main square where all the hotels and paved roads were. That was not the case. My face dropped when the bus driver informed me that this was the end of the line. What the…?

It was a dark dirt road in the middle of nowhere with no taxis, hotels or signs of life. Are you freaking serious? Were we being punked? Where was the hidden camera?

Thankfully I was not alone. A handsome backpacker from New Zealand and two girls from Holland were also abandoned on the side of the road. The four of headed towards town making our way through the muddy streets. This was twice as difficult for me as I had to drag my suitcase – the others had backpacks.

Dragging my suitcase through the muddy streets of San Pedro in the middle of the night looking for a hotel room was not fun.

Chile is supposed to be one of the most developed countries in South America and their main tourist town does not even have paved roads. What the…? Even cities over 2000 years old like Pompeii have paved roads.

▲ *The sidewalks in San Pedro are so narrow that most people end up walking on the road.*

▲ *The majority of San Pedro is covered with dirt roads, which turn to mud when it rains.*

When we reached the main square, which was made out of paving stones, it proved that they were in fact aware of the technology. So why the heck didn't they use it for the rest of the town? I just don't understand how they could live that way. In my calculations dirt roads = bad and paved roads = good. In their defence, they did have paved sidewalks but they were so narrow that most people ended up walking on the roads.

The others had already booked accommodations but I didn't. I had anticipated arriving at 4:00 pm which would have given me plenty of daytime to find something. Since it was a popular tourist town I figured they must have wall to wall hotels and hostels. I parted ways with the group when I found a hostel on the square. I went in to inquire about a room only to discover they were booked solid. Making my way down the dark muddy streets I came across two other places that were also booked solid. By the time I reached the fourth hotel only to find it also had no vacancies, I broke into tears.

I did not have another minute of *dragging my suitcase through the mud in the dark looking for a room* left in me.

The kind man at the reception desk took pity on me and promised he would find me a room while I sat with his female friend sipping warm coca tea.

That is when I discovered that I had landed in Chile's busiest tourist city in the middle of their high season on a Saturday night – not the greatest time to drop in looking for a room. Woops.

The woman was surprised to discover I was a travel writer. She had expected me to have done a little research before I arrived but I told her I was not that organized. I had only heard of the city a few days before and preferred to book my rooms in person so I could see what I was getting. She was shocked that this method worked and that I never ended up sleeping on the street. Despite the fact that I worry about dumb stuff all the time, I always trust the Universe to find me a hotel room.

▲ *San Pedro's church is located in the main square which is the only paved part of the city.*

I had barely sipped my tea when the man returned with a big smile and the key to a room at the hostel down the street. He was even kind enough to walk me over and carry my guitar. I get to meet some of the nicest people in my travels who have helped me out of some real binds. This helps remind me of how many wonderful and caring people there are in the world.

The room was bare bones but it was in my price range and I was lucky enough to get it for two nights. Things were definitely starting to look up for Teresa the traveler.

First thing the next morning I walked into a travel agency and that's where I met Rocco, a energetic man in his 60's with a penchant for beautiful women – a category in which he placed me. <Blush>

In between his cheesy lines and compliments, he informed me that this was the most rain the area had seen in years…great if I had come to town to mud wrestle but unfortunately that was not the nature of my visit.

Because of the rain, many tours were not available as they required the trucks to traverse rivers which were now too high. Most backpackers were getting out of dodge and heading to Bolivia.

He suggested I do the same and when he told me that I could see much of the same things in Bolivia as I could in Chile such as pink flamingos, salt lakes and geysers…all for much cheaper, I was sold.

He directed me to a bank machine that took visa – a necessity I was not able to find on my own – and I paid him in cash then returned to my room. Being a Virgo, I am a neat freak so needless to say I was not inspired to venture out on the streets of San Pedro for any reason other than to eat dinner. Despite the fact the town had some nice cafes and courtyards; I wasn't able to get over the lack of pavement and could not wait to make my escape. I spent the rest of the day in bed which was exactly what I needed to get over my sinus cold and reserve energy for my three-day desert tour.

▲ *The inside of San Pedro's church is very rustic with wooden floors and a wooden ceiling.*

Top Ten Crazy Chile Facts

1. The international spotlight was on Chile in 2010 when 33 miners were trapped in a collapsed mine for over two months. They were rescued that same year on October 13th during a dramatic rescue effort that had the entire world sitting at the edge of their seats.
2. Chile's Atacama Desert is the world's most arid desert but I would have never guessed that when I was there…record rainfall had turned it into a mud bog.
3. Chile is Latin America's first first-world nation.
4. Many tour operators and hostels prefer to be paid in cash.
5. I only spent two days there so I am in no way an expert on the country.
6. With 2,700 miles of coastline, Chile has one of the longest coastlines in the world.
7. David Selkirk, better known as Robinson Crusoe, survived a shipwreck and lived for several years on a desert island off the coast of Chile.
8. There are 2000 volcanoes in Chile of which 50 are active.
9. Chile elected its first female president, Michelle Bachelet Jeria in 2006. She served from March 11th 2006 until March 11th 2010.
10. English is mandatory for students in public school attending grades five and above.

What Did Things Cost?

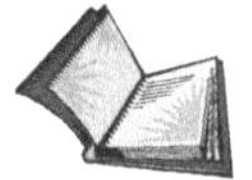

Items Purchased	Chile Pesos	American Dollars
Bus from Salta to San Pedro De Atacama	25,000	$50.00
Single room with shared bathroom in hostel	20,000	$40.00
Internet café 15 minutes	200	$0.40
Three day two night desert and salt flat tour	70,000	$140.00
Small bottle of water	600	$1.20
Tasteless chicken Caesar salad	10,000	$20.00
Hippy Pants	16,000	$32.00

Bolivian Mud Flats

First thing in the morning I dragged my luggage through the muddy streets of San Pedro for the last time and waited at the pickup location for the bus and that's where I met Mickey and Sarah – a couple from Ireland. On the bus we met a couple from France and a girl from Turkey and, since the six of us were the only English speaking people on the t, by the time we reached the Bolivian boarder we had become fast friends.

The Bolivian immigration office was modest to say the least. Considering Bolivia is one of the least developed countries in South America with over two-thirds of its people living in poverty, I guess this was to be expected.

After we had our passports stamped, a group of Bolivian tour guides, each driving a Land Cruiser, met us at the border where we split up into groups of six for the remainder of the tour. Needless to say, the six of us migrated to the same vehicle. I was thankful to be in an all-English speaking group…it is not as much fun when I'm not able to communicate well with the other people on my tour.

▲ *Our group of six entered Bolivia fully prepared to have a great time.*

We drove from the border to the entrance to Eduardo Avaroa National Park where we purchased our passes before visiting the White Lagoon for our first glimpse at the beautiful pink flamingos that inhabit all of the desert's lagoons including the Laguna Verde, Laguna Altiplanicas and Laguna Colorada.

The geysers Sol de Manana were one of my favorite sights on the first day. Despite their name they are not in fact geysers rather they are part of a geothermal field extending over an area of 10 km². The sulfur springs field consists of mud lakes and steam pools of boiling mud. Several holes, which are referred to as geysers, emit the pressurized steam, however a true geyser emits water. Unfortunately the cold wind and rain prevented us from spending too much time at this magnificent site.

Johnny Cash Bonding Moment

Day one ended around 4 pm when we pulled up to a hostel nestled beside yet another lagoon filled with pink flamingos.

Rocco had warned us that the accommodations for the first night would be pretty rough but I had no idea just how rough they would be. The six of us all had to share a room with no heat and barely any electricity save for a single dull light bulb. The French couple shared a rickety bunk bed that squeaked all night while the rest of us got single beds covered with heavy red and yellow children's bedspreads with pictures of teddy bears and elephants. The coed shared bathroom had three toilets that did not flush. Toilet paper was to be thrown in a trash can and people were required to fill a jug with water and pour it into the toilet until your deposit disappeared. It looked and smelled nasty and did not come with a shower…not that I would ever want to take shower there.

I knew it was going to be a cold uncomfortable night and it was starting to get me down. I needed to find a way to lift my spirits and entertain myself for the evening without the luxury of internet or television. After dinner, the group was sitting in the cold dining room drinking beer when it occurred to me this was the perfect time to pull out my travel guitar. I had been dragging it around for over a month and barely played it. I was starting to regret my decision to bring it along.

Considering we were from all over the world, I had no idea what songs people would recognize. I sang some Kid Rock and Poison but no one sang along.

One of my favorite all-time artists is the late-great Man in Black Johnny Cash so I decided to share his music with the group starting with my rendition of *Folsom Prison Blues*. I certainly wasn't expecting anyone to know it. I had sung it all over the world to everyone from Camel herders in the Sahara Desert to the owners of a Vietnamese restaurant in Venice. No one outside of Canada and the United States had ever sung along.

So you can imagine my surprise when the couple from Ireland shouted out Johnny Cash and joined in. Moments later we were joined by two young Chilean guys, the French couple and the Turkish girl. OMG…I was in heaven. JOHNNY CASH HEAVEN!

Never in my wildest dreams did I imagine that one day I would be staying at a crappy hostel in the middle of the Bolivian desert singing Johnny Cash songs with a bunch of fellow fans from all over the world. Talk about stepping into a big pile of happy.

▲ *The geysers Sol de Manana are not actually geysers they are steam vents in a geothermal field.*

We wrapped up the sing-a-long with a round of *Walk the Line* followed by *Ring of Fire* and by the time we went to sleep our group and the six people from the other Land Cruiser had bonded into one big Johnny Cash loving family. One of my favorite sayings is, "it's not the number of breaths you take but the number of moments that take your breath away" and this was one of those moments.

Rabbit Tales

I spent the entire first day occupying the front seat which was by far the best seat in the truck but by the second day I felt it was only fair to offer it up to someone else.

The Frenchman, who was an avid photographer, jumped at the chance leaving me in the backseat near the window. Unfortunately the knob on the window was broken so I was not able to roll it down to snap pictures leaving me wish I had chosen the other side. I hate it when I do that…think that someone else has a better seat, a better meal, or a better whatever than me. I imagine being happier if I had what they had and then I just end up feeling unhappy. Why can't I just be happy with what I have?

I decided to just be happy where I was and trust that the Universe placed me there for a reason and that is when it happened. The Land Cruiser in front of us stopped in the middle of a gorge forcing us to stop as well. Looking out the window I noticed people taking pictures of two rabbit-like creatures.

They were a combination between a rabbit and a chinchilla with long ears and long tails. I had seen a pack of them in the Argentinean desert but was not able to get close. I also spotted one at Machu Picchu but it also eluded my lens. This was my big opportunity.

Since I couldn't roll down my window to take a decent picture, I opened the door and crouched down to the ground. Seconds later the animals disappeared up the cliff and hid in the rocks leaving me without a single shot. The Frenchman in the front seat was able to get plenty of good shots while I got none making me feel even worse about having to sit in the back. I gave myself a mental slap upside the head and reminded myself that everything happens for a reason and it's usually a good one.

I was just about to admit defeat and return to my seat when suddenly one of the rabbits hopped back and stopped right in front of me posing nicely with its front paws on a rock and stayed until I got the perfect shot. Then it came right up to me and sniffed my hand perhaps hoping he would be rewarded. Unfortunately I had nothing to give him which is a good thing because we all know it is not good to feed wildlife as it puts them and us in danger. But it would have been hard to resist.

▲ *The Land Cruisers were able to make it through deep bogs with no problems.*

That was one of the best moments in my tour and it reminded me to be happy with where I am at and what I have. In other words, the grass isn't always greener on the other side and if it is who cares?

Mud Flats

We were supposed to watch the sun set over the salt flats on day two but because of all the rain the road had turned into mud forcing us to drive to Uyuni instead. The majority of the day was spent driving through the small lakes that had formed on the dirt road and helping to push vehicles out of the mud. We came across one that had been stuck for over two hours.

At first I was frustrated by the slow pace and constant challenges. Our vehicle broke down twice forcing us to wait on the side of the road for almost an hour while our guide and another driver fixed it. Something I severely lack is patience. I am usually so busy racing from place to place that I rarely slow down and just be.

I think the Universe was trying to teach me something so I took a deep breath and released all my attachment to getting anywhere fast and decided to sit back and let the events of the day unfold without feeling anxious about it.

I looked down at the silver dog tag on my backpack with a quote from Albert Einstein that reads, "In the midst of difficulty lies opportunity" and waited to see what opportunities would arise.

Once I relaxed, I discovered that the roadside stops were kind of fun. It gave me the opportunity to get to know people. During one of the stops I had a chance to get to know a guy from Chile who had the same camera as me and on another stop I met an interesting German guy who was traveling solo on a motorbike across South America. He and his bike travelled over from Germany on a cargo ship that took four weeks to get to port. I could not imagine spending four weeks on a cargo ship unless the crew consisted of Chippendale dancers and massage therapists. He became our "Where's Waldo" for the remainder of the trip. We spotted him everywhere: in the small villages where we stopped to eat, on the salt flats, at our hotel in Uyuni and in the pub where we stopped for drinks before catching the bus to La Paz. By dinner that night, the 12 of us who had been traveling in two Land Cruisers together had become good friends and isn't that what traveling is all about…making new friends?

▲ *A flock of pink flamingos grazing in a lagoon*

When Monique had returned to Canada I felt alone not trusting in my ability to make new friends and here I was, part of an international group of backpackers feeling like I had known them for years.

With each passing day my depression lifted and I started to feel like a better version of my old self. I was having the time of my life and it was all because the Universe forced me to slow down and be where I was at. And where I was at was in the middle of a muddy desert in Bolivia. Who knew that's where I would find my happy? Chances are I would lose it again but I was confident that if I forced myself to slow down and be where I am at, it would catch up to me. Wow…my confidence had returned.

Pink Flamingos

One of my favourite parts of our tour was the animal sightings. The desert was rich with wildlife especially pink flamingos, vicunas and viscachas.

Having grown up in a middle-class blue-collar Canadian neighbourhood I of course saw my fair share of lawns decorated with plastic pink flamingos.

In fact, the first thing I did when I finally owned my own lawn was decorate it with those pink plastic birds. Over the years I had seen many a pink flamingo in captivity but never dreamed I would see one in the wild so when I roamed the streets of San Pedro looking to book a tour of the Bolivian desert you can imagine my delight when I saw pictures of flamingo filled lagoons. I had no idea there were flamingos in Bolivia.

Pink flamingos are not actually born pink. They are grey and turn pink as they grow older as a result of a diet consisting of shrimp and plankton high in carotenoid proteins.

▶ *From top to bottom: Viscacha – a rabbit-looking rodent related to the chinchilla, three vicunas which are related to the llama, a loon and a pink flamingo walking across a lagoon.*

Their oddly shaped beaks separate the mud and silt from their food allowing them to filter feed.

After two days of stopping at lagoons filled with thousands of pink flamingos they no longer excited me. Can you believe I actually became bored with this fascinating bird? They are as common to the Bolivian desert as pigeons are to town squares.

Thankfully our vicuna sighting broke up the monotony. The vicuna is a camelids which lives in the alpine areas of the Andes. Related to the llama, it is believed to be the wild ancestor of the domesticated alpacas which are raised for their fine wool. The Inca valued the vicunas for their wool but since the animals could only be shorn once every three years, only royalty was allowed to wear vicuna garments.

Being a rabbit-lover, my favourite encounter was with a viscacha. While it resembles a rabbit with its long ears, the viscacha is actually related to the chinchilla.

Rain is a Good Thing

The next day we were relieved to learn that the roads were open and we would make it out to the Salar de Uyuni.

At 10,582 square kilometres and 3,656 meters above sea level, it is the world's largest salt flat. It was formed as a result of transformations between several prehistoric lakes which over the centuries dried up and became covered with a few meters of salt crust. Beneath the crust is a 2 to 20 meter deep pool of brine that is rich in lithium containing 50%, to 70% of the world's reserves. Because of its large area which can be seen from space, and its exceptional flatness, it is the ideal object for calibrating the altimeters of the Earth observation satellites. In the center of the Salar there are a few islands which are actually the tops of ancient volcanoes.

Despite the world demand for lithium, from which batteries are made, the Bolivian government isn't allowing exploitation by foreign corporations which is probably a wise thing. The locals, despite being poor, were concerned that none of the profits from the mining activity would reach them and were probably right. The Bolivian government plans to build its own pilot plant with a modest annual production of 1,200 tons to be increased over time.

As the Salar began to attract tourists from around the world, hotels made entirely from salt blocks cut from the Salar began to spring up. The first, which was completed in 1995 and located in the middle of the salt flat, was dismantled in 2002 due to mismanagement leading to environmental problems. Most of the waste had to be collected manually but wasn't. Instead the raw sewerage was being pumped directly into the Salar. The new salt hotels were built closer to the roads and in full compliance with environmental codes.

Despite the fact the Salar is not very far from the town of Uyuni, it still took us a few hours to get there because of poor road conditions and a pit stop at one of the tiny muddy towns along the way. Pavement is not a common sight in this part of Bolivia and the heavy rains of the past few days had transformed the land around the salt flats into one huge mud flat. I had to go to the bathroom during our pit stop so I picked my way across the muddy market and followed a sign that said bano to a little shack manned by an old man with a deeply creased face. For 2 Bolivianos he sold me a few sheets of pink toilet paper and directed me to the washroom. I use that term loosely because this was not even close to something I would call a washroom. One of the key ingredients in washrooms is a toilet and I did not consider this hole in the ground with two footholds a toilet.

Despite the fact I have used these before in Central America and the Middle East I have still not mastered the technique. I ended up peeing on my shoe as I often do. When I returned to the Land Cruiser, I complained to the group about my harrowing bathroom experience and the Turkish girl replied, "They gave you toilet paper?" Apparently she ended up at a different bathroom that did not offer toilet paper and was given a stick to wedge in the door to keep it shut. The French couple added that the worst bathroom they had used was in China. The line of holes in the ground was not even separated by walls. Going to the John was a social event. Yikes!

Suddenly my bathroom experience didn't seem so bad after all. My door had a lock, the wall had a mirror and a hook for your jacket and I got to wipe in private with pretty pink toilet paper. I guess my glass was half full and not half empty as I had thought.

The road to the salt flats was riddled with potholes and I know that for a fact because I felt each one we hit. However, there is always someone worse off and that day it was the Irish couple who sat in the small raised seat at the very back. By the time we reached the edge of the Salar, the Irishman claimed his neck was now two inches shorter and he was hoping it would pop back out soon.

When we got out of the truck and caught our first chilly glimpse of the Salar, it was nothing to write home about. The sky was socked in turning the salt flats into a white abyss.

▲ *Some of the public bathrooms in Bolivia are modest to say the least.*

Is this it? I spent two days driving across the muddy desert and sleeping in crappy hostels for this! What the..? I wanted my money back…this sucked. We piled back into the Land Cruiser but rather than head back to Uyuni we drove out onto the salt flats until we reached what I immediately recognized as a salt hotel in the middle of the flats. I had thought they built them along the shoreline not right in the middle.

We entered a building made entirely of salt and sat at a salt table where we drank a beer. I decided this wasn't so bad after all and began to have fun chatting with other tourists from around the world while the rain tapped down on the tin roof. Then suddenly it stopped. Could it be?

I walked outside and much to my delight the sun was shining and the clouds had separated allowing patches of blue sky to peak through. The rain had left a 2-inch layer of water across the flats which mirrored the sky creating a scene that looked like heaven.

People began to trickle out of the hotel and walk across the flats to admire this incredible sight and take that perfect, "I am in heaven" picture.

▲ *When covered with water the Salar becomes the world's largest mirror.*

I was suddenly thankful for the rain that I had been cursing all morning. The Luke Bryan song Rain is a Good Thing played in my head.

My daddy spent his life
Lookin' up at the sky
He'd cuss, kick the dust,
Sayin' son it's way too dry
It clouds up in the city,
The weather man complains
But where I come from,
Rain is a good thing
Rain makes corn,
Corn makes whiskey
Whiskey makes my baby
Feel a little frisky

Back roads are boggin' up,
My buddies pile up in my truck
We hunt our honeys down,
We take 'em into town
Start washin' all our worries
Down the drain
Rain is a good thing

Rain was a good thing. So good that it inspired my best happy dance and I convinced the rest of the people on the Salt Flat to join me. I really was in heaven. As we drove back to Uyuni on the pothole ridden muddy roads I thought to myself, my Salar experience could not have been more perfect.

Popcorn Popper

Hoping to escape the muddy streets of Uyuni, the six of us bought tickets for the overnight bus to La Paz leaving at 5pm and arriving at 5am. Unlike the buses in Canada, with set schedules that are generally met, the buses of Bolivia are not as reliable. We arrived at 4:45pm only to be informed that due to poor ticket sales, the bus would not be leaving until 8 forcing us to kill 3 hours in the pub. The Irish couple didn't seem to mind.

As promised the bus left at 8pm for the wildest overnight bus ride in history. The six of us occupied the entire back half of the bus each getting our own row.

▲ *A number of salt hotels constructed entirely of salt blocks cut from the Salar are located on the flats.*

Sprawled out across two seats, the gentle vibration of the bus driving along the highway would usually put me to sleep. However, the highways in this part of Bolivia lacked a very important ingredient: pavement. Yes you read that right – the highway was made out of dirt that quickly turned to mud with all the rain.

It wasn't long before our bus got stuck and remained stuck for almost four hours while the driver and a group of villagers attempted to push us out. Finally a large truck arrived and pulled us out much to the relief of all the buses and transport trucks lined up behind us.

Once back on the road we picked up speed and flew out of our seats knocking our heads on the ceiling each time we hit a pothole – the road was riddled with them. I felt like I was riding inside a hot-air popcorn popper. The 12- hour trip turned into a 17-hour ride from hell so needless to say we all breathed a huge sigh of relieve when we arrived in La Paz the following day in one piece but smelling pretty ripe to say the least.

We parted ways with the French couple at the bus station. They already had a hostel booked and were planning to leave the next morning on a two-week guided trek in the mountains. These avid climbers thought nothing of camping in the cold wet mountains for weeks at a time without hot showers and comfy beds. They are what you call low-maintenance people. I am what you call high-maintenance, if I go too long without a hot shower and a comfortable bed, I have a breakdown. I could already feel one coming on and knew I had to check into a nice hotel pronto. The Irish couple, the Turkish girl and I had a taxi drop us off in San Pedro square and there we found the perfect hotel in which to recover from our overnight bus extravaganza.

The following day, after picking up our laundry the others went to the bus station to purchase their tickets for Lake Titicaca while I spent the day on my own contemplating what I wanted to do next. I was feeling a little travelled-out and felt it was time to start heading home.

▲ *A Bolivian couple goes for a stroll on the large green catwalk that offers the best views of the city.*

But before I returned to the blanket of snow covering my hometown I wanted to spend some time on a sunny beach so I could at least return with a tan...but where? I needed to go somewhere that West Jet flew so I could fly home using the buddy passes my friend gave me.

Miami Beach Body

While I was booking my trip to South America an advertisement kept popping up that said fly to Orlando. In fact before I left on my trip I kept noticing the name Orlando and wondered if the Universe was trying to tell me something. Orlando was the home of Disney World and no doubt a happy warm place so I went online to see if West Jet flew there and much to my delight they did.

However, when I tried to book my flight through Travelocity they would not accept my credit card. How odd…I had booked all my flights to that point through them and never had a problem. Instead I visited the travel agency next to my hotel to see if I could book a flight with them.

When the agent told me I would have to fly to Miami first then change planes to get to Orlando it occurred to me that Miami has a world famous beach. What better place to work on my tan? Orlando could wait.

After I booked my trip to Miami I put on my bikini and stood in front of the mirror to take stock and determine how beach-ready I was. Much to my surprise I noticed how trim and sculpted my new physique was. Five weeks of sand-boarding, exploring Inca ruins, climbing the steps to my hotel rooms, walking the city streets, repelling down a waterfall and eating sensibly had finally paid off. For the first time in a long time I loved my reflection. I looked so happy and healthy. Was this really me?

Knowing how I was struggling to feel comfortable in my own skin, Monique sent me an email after she returned home that said, "You will walk by a mirror in the very near future and see your reflection and say wow there I am. Then you will be all right I promise.

▶ *It is a Bolivian tradition to bury a dried llama fetus in the foundations of new construction.*

▲ *Amulets of lovers are purchased to improve sex life, combat impotency and increase fertility.*

When I was finally able to tear myself away from my own reflection I spot checked my armpits and legs wondering if I needed to shave. Much to my surprise very little hair had grown back. I think if was afraid to after that painful Peruvian waxing. Wouldn't that be nice?

Love Potion #10

After my friends left for Peru I thought I would be all alone in La Paz, but that was not the case. A girl from Germany who I had met at the Flying Dog Hostel in Arequipa had just arrived in town and sent me a message on Facebook inviting me to visit the Witches Market. Witches Market, what the…?

I did a little research and discovered that the market, which is also known as El Mercado de las Brujas, was not only popular with the locals it also attracted tourists from all over the world. Located on Calle Jiminez and Linares between Sagarnaga and Santa Cruz, this is the place to go if you are looking for potions, dried herbs and seeds, soapstone amulets, dried snakes and frogs, aphrodisiac formulas and dried llama fetuses.

Yes, you read that right, they sell a large assortment of dried llama fetuses. These are purchased by the poor as an offering to the goddess Pachamama (Mother Earth) and buried in the foundations of new construction. The wealthier Bolivians are expected to sacrifice a live llama. It is estimated that 99% of Bolivian families have a dried llama fetus thrown under the foundations of their house for luck.

To ensure success in a new business venture, a dried llama fetus is burned on a plate of sweets and herbs, to strike it rich one should stick a cigarette in the mouth of a dried frog, if you place a dried armadillo at the entrance to your house it will prevent thieves from entering. An amulette d'amor will ensure you get hitched while a naked ceramic couple will improve your sex life, cure impotency and increase fertility.

▲ *I picked up love amulets for me and all my single friends in the hopes that we would all be in happy relationships by the end of the year.*

As we wound our way through the bustling narrow streets, we came across a number of stores selling soapstone amulets unfortunately we had no idea what they were for until we found a store with signs posted in English explaining the significance of each one.

Two of the amulets jumped out at me: the sun which was for happiness and prosperity and the love amulets so I purchased a sun and a couple in a lover's embrace.

After I had already paid, I noticed a different love amulet - a happy couple arm in arm with a heart between them. I looked at the two carefully to determine which kind of love I really wanted. The lovers amulet was one I was all too familiar with. Heaven knows I have had my share of steamy relationships where the sex was great but after a short time it fizzled out.

The happy couple was foreign to me, I don't ever recall being in that kind of relationship. They looked so secure and happy….that was what I wanted. Before I left I quickly tossed the lovers back into the basket from which they came and placed the happy couple into my backpack.

Realizing I had a number of single friends who also wanted to be part of a happy couple, I returned the next day and bought love amulets for all and also picked up the lovers amulet for myself deciding that I wanted it all: passion and contentment.

Follow your happy – Teresa the Traveler

▲ *Our favourite pose in the desert was the jump.*

Top Ten Crazy Bolivia Facts

1. The world's largest dinosaur footprints are found near the Bolivian city of Sucre. Declared a UNESCO site, there are over 5000 tracks made by up to 150 dinosaurs estimated to be nearly 70-million years old with the largest prints measuring over three feet in length.
2. It is believed that Butch Cassidy and the Sundance Kid were killed in a shootout with the Bolivian army in San Vicente after robbing the payroll of a mining company in Tupiza. Buried in the small San Vicente cemetery are the bodies of what some believe are the two bandits however, DNA tests done in 1991 by a team of scientists did not match that of their living relatives.
3. Lake Titicaca, on the boarder of Bolivia and Peru, is the highest navigable lake in the world.
4. The world's largest deposit of lithium, used to manufacture batteries, is located underneath the salt flats but mining it would destroy Bolivia's number one tourist attraction the Salar de Uyuni.
5. The Cerro Mutun located near Santa Cruz is the world's largest iron ore mine. It is run by Jindel, a company based in India.
6. The world's largest butterfly sanctuary is located in Santa Cruz.
7. Bolivia is home to the worlds only known Boliviana mine – a yellow and purple precious stone produces when citrine and ametrine combine.
8. Potosi is the highest city in the world and La Paz is the second highest.
9. From 1557 to 1985, the mining industry dominated the Bolivian economy.
10. The women wrap everything from groceries to children inside brightly colored blankets and carry them on their backs.

▲ *Our tour group at the Salt Hotel*

▲ *The Bolivian desert is a landscape photographer's dream come true.*

What Did Things Cost?

Items Purchased	Bolivia Bolivianos	American Dollars
Entrance to Eduardo Avaroa Reserve	150.00	$20.00
Bus from Uyuni to La Paz	100.00	$13.50
Single room in Uyuni	80.00	$10.80
Public bathroom	1.00	$0.13
Dinner in Uyuni	40.00	$5.40
Lunch (pizza and drinks) in La Paz	50.00	$7.00
Single room in nice hotel in La Paz	266.00	$38.00
Short taxi ride in La Paz	10.00	$1.40
Love amulet at witch market	3.00	$0.40
Larger sun amulet to hang on my wall	15.00	$2.10
Laundry and lots of it	80.00	$11.40
Taxi to airport	50.00	$7.10

Miami Beach Babe

When I purchased my ticket from the American Airlines office I specifically asked for a window seat. I always ask for a window or isle seat because I am claustrophobic and go crazy when I have to sit between two people. Even at the movie theatre I have to sit near the isle, I am not sure why but it has something to do with being able to make a quick escape. From what I have no idea.

Murphy Law sucks! As I was standing in line to board the plane I noticed I had been assigned a middle seat. I was not a happy camper. But instead of working myself into an anxiety attack, I decided to sit down, take a deep breath and trust that things would work themselves out. I figured that if I was the last on the plane I could ask the stewardess to relocate me…perhaps if there were no seats left in economy she would be forced to seat me in first class where there is almost always empty seats.

I told myself to look at it as an opportunity then obviously sat there in quiet contemplation for too long because a man walked up to me and said are you Teresa Cline? When I replied yes, he said the plane was waiting for me. What the…? There was still a huge line-up of people how could that be. Apparently they were boarding a different flight at the same gate. Nothing makes sense in South America.

I explained my conundrum and while I was getting my carryon bags searched once again (American Airlines does a final search just before you board the plane) the man was looking into a solution. He came back with my new seat assignment: the front of the plane by the exit doors. Wow…I had more leg room than I have legs. It was perfect! I love it when my problems solve themselves without me having to do anything. Thanks Universe!

▲ *South Beach is the most popular tourist area of Miami.*

A little tip for you travelers, a pilot told me that a plane cannot legally take off without you if it has your luggage onboard. Before they can depart they must either remove your luggage or find you. It is usually quicker to find the passenger so they will make the effort.

Valentine's Day Massacre

I think I pissed St. Valentine off when I was younger because he's been biting me in the butt ever since. I was in grade 9 the first time I ever received flowers from a guy. A boy I had met at the roller rink developed a crush on me and decided to win my heart by sending me a dozen roses on Valentine's Day.

When my name was called over the loud speakers with instructions for me to go to the office I thought for sure I was in trouble…yet again.

Instead the secretary handed me a huge bouquet of red roses with a love letter attached telling me a handsome boy asked her to deliver them to me. OMG…I was mortified. I wasn't even sure if I liked this guy and here he was making his feelings known in front of all my high school peers.

Thankfully he delivered them at the end of the day so I didn't have to carry them around all day as they were too big to fit into my locker. I, of course, got teased all the way home by the other kids on the bus and later that night when he called me I told him I never wanted to see him again…poor guy.

Three years later I received my second bouquet of flowers from a guy on Valentine's Day. I was working at a law firm as their Girl Friday when a courier dropped off an enormous arrangement of yellow, pink and blue flowers along with a love letter from the guy I had been dating for the past year. The guy had cheated on me countless times until I finally had enough and sent him a Valentine's Card with a Dear John letter attached. He obviously sent the flowers before he received my card.

I'm pretty sure that was the last time I got flowers from a guy on Valentine's Day with the exception of the time I was working in Cold Lake at a large construction site. I was one of only four women that worked on the site of 800 men and some of the men were kind enough to chip in and buy us flowers for Valentine's Day. When I was called into the office I thought I was in trouble as usual but instead my boss handed me flowers. Life can be so unpredictable.

February 14th is a cursed day for me. I have usually been single and the few times I did have a boyfriend we were not able to spend it together because I was working out of town. Needless to say, I hate Valentine's Day. It's a time for lovers to celebrate their love while we terminally single people feel bad about not yet having met our true love. If I ever meet St. Valentine I am going to bitch slap him…no I'm not. Each year I secretly hope that this year will be different. That this will be the year I get whisked away on a romantic weekend by the man of my dreams. Then I wake up. Reality can really suck sometimes.

Why am I so attached to having a fairy tale ending? When will I just be happy with the way things are and give up these silly school girl fantasies?

I would had forgotten about Valentine's Day all together if it wasn't for all my Facebook friends who posted happy V-Day on their statuses and changed their profile pictures to hearts and cupids. At least I was on a plane to Miami feeling lousy instead of sitting at home feeling lousy. Or worse yet, out with all my single friends at a pub pretending to be happily single. The in-flight chick flick with the airport ending wasn't doing anything to help. Why do these movies all end with someone racing through traffic to get to the airport to stop their lover from boarding a plane? Predictably they get there just in time only to realize their lover didn't get on the plane after all…they were back at (insert location here) waiting for them. Someone please come up with a new ending.

I hoped my pity party would end by the time we landed in Miami because I really wanted to have some fun in the sun before returning to cold Kamloops.

Seventies Porn Room

One thing I love about visiting the United States is how easy everything is. After waiting in long immigration lines at pretty much every border crossing, I was delighted to discover a long line of immigration officers waiting for us when we got off the plane. Within minutes I had my passport stamped and was outside the airport looking for a cab. As I stood in the taxi line, I was handed a Miami tourist book complete with a city map. Again…how convenient is that?

I shared a cab to South Beach with Salty Bob, a tall 60-something year old ship captain from the Caribbean who reminded me of a swinger from the 70's. His shirt was unbuttoned just enough to liberate his chest hair while his gold chain and his year-round tan screamed, "Groovy baby". Bob's friend, who had just passed away, owned a number of boutique hotels in South Beach where he had partied away many a night. He explained that the theme in the area was art deco and he was right. When I walked into my room it felt like I had just stepped onto the set of a 70's porn flick.

The stark white walls were accented by a huge white and red padded headboard, the ceiling was decorated with large red polka dots and the furniture was mirrored to match the huge mirror on the bathroom door and the stand up mirror in the corner.

I liked the room but I did not like the noise. The lobby had a lounge with a DJ spinning the latest house music at full blast from noon until the wee hours of the morning. Each room alsocame equipped with its own stereo. Sleep was a commodity in this place.

Florida Everglades

The first thing I did after settling into my room was book a tour of the Everglades for the following day. Since hearing John Anderson's song *Seminole Wind*, I have been fascinated with the area.

Ever since the days of old
Men would search for wealth untold.
They'd dig for silver and for gold,
and leave the empty holes.
And way down south
In the Everglades,
Where the black water rolls
And the saw grass waves.
The eagles fly and the otters play,
In the land of the Seminole.

So blow, blow Seminole wind,
Blow like you're never
gonna blow again.
I'm calling to you
Like a long lost friend,
But I know who you are.
And blow, blow from the Okeechobee,
All the way up to Micanopy.
Blow across the home of the Seminole,

The alligators and the garr.

Progress came and took its toll,
And in the name of flood control,
They made their plans and they drained the land,
Now the glades are going dry.
And the last time
I walked in the swamp,
I sat upon a Cypress stump,
I listened close and I heard the ghost,
Of Osceola cry.

The Everglades are a subtropical wetland starting in Orlando, Florida. The Kissimee River discharges into the vast yet shallow Lake Okeechobee forming a slow moving river 60 miles wide and over 100 miles long flowing southward across a limestone shelf to Florida Bay. Named for the sawgrass blades that seem to go on forever, the Everglades was inhabited 15,000 years ago by the Calusa and Tequesta tribes whose population declined in the 16th century after the Spanish arrived.

After the Seminole Wars of the 19th century, the Seminoles were forced by the US military to live in the Everglades.

The Seminole Wars, also known as the Florida Wars were three conflicts that took place in the time frame of 1817 to 1858 between various groups of Native Americans collectively known as the Seminoles, and the United States Army. Many of the Seminoles were bribed to move west while others were forced to leave or killed in the wars. By the end of the third war there were only around 100 Seminoles left in Florida.

Today the Seminole remain a part of the Everglades where they serve as a tourist attraction wrestling alligators and running souvenir stands. They also run casinos to support the six remaining Seminole reservations in Florida. The Everglade's fragile ecosystem was first threatened by drainage in 1882, in an effort to develop the land. Around 1,400 miles of canals, levees and water control devices were constructed to divert the water to the cities and portions were transformed into farmland to grow primarily sugarcane.

With approximately 50 percent of the original Everglades turned into farmland and urban areas, it wasn't until the 1970's when international attention turned to the environmental crisis of the area and it was designated as one of only three wetland areas of global importance. Restoration efforts were launched in the 1980's to preserve the Everglades.

There are six different ecosystems that make up the Everglades including: sawgrass marshes and sloughs, tropical hardwood hammock, pineland, cypress, mangrove and coastal prairie and Florida Bay.

The sawgrass marshes are the primary feature of the Everglades. This is where the crocodiles nest and where aquatic animals such as turtles, alligators, snakes and fish thrive, as well as a number of bird species.

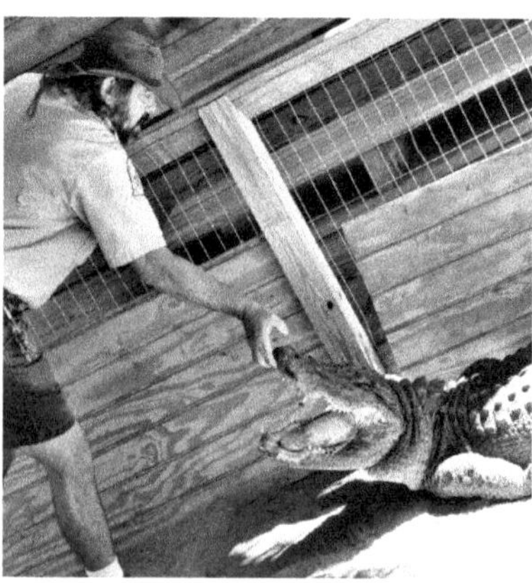

▲ *Most Everglade tours end with a crocodile show.*

▲ *Since the Everglades are so shallow, airboats are used to navigate them.*

Small islands of trees called tropical hardwood hammocks grow on land raised between 1-3 feet above the sloughs and prairies. While they are difficult for humans to penetrate, they make ideal habitats for small mammals, reptiles and amphibians.

The driest land in the Everglades, located at the highest altitude, is called pineland. This area relies on fire for its survival as it burns off the competing vegetation on the forest floor and opens pine cones to germinate seeds. A period without significant fire can transform pineland into a hardwood hammock as the larger trees overtake the slash pines.

Cypress swamps are also found throughout the Everglades with the largest being the Big Cypress Swamp located west of the sawgrass prairies.

Mangrove trees, which grow in oxygen-poor soil, are tolerant of salt and can survive drastic changes in water levels, protect the coastline during severe storms by absorbing the energy of waves and storm surges. Most are located in the transitional zone where fresh water meets salt water. In fact, the Everglades have the most extensive system of mangroves in the world. Since there is no boarder between the coastal marshes and Florida Bay, it is considered to be part of the Everglade watershed. There are approximately 100 keys (islands) many of which are mangrove forests. The fresh water flowing into the bay creates the perfect conditions for vast beds of turtle grass and algae formations to thrive. These are the foundations for animal life in the bay, which is home to sea turtles and manatees.

With the environment being threatened, a number of initiatives have been put in place to restore the wetlands, which act as filters for pollution, and improve the quality of water. The Comprehensive Everglades Restoration Plan, first authorized by congress in 1948, provides a framework for restoring and preserving the water resources of central and southern Florida. It proposed over 60 construction projects over 30 years designed to better store and manage the water.

Despite support from President Clinton in 2000, the plan has received little in the way of federal funds as most of the money has already been spent in the war with Iraq. The State of Florida, however, reports having spent over 2 billion on various projects including over 36,000 acres of storm water treatment areas constructed to filter 2,500 short tons of phosphorus from the waters of the Everglades.

In 2008, the State of Florida also agreed to buy U.S. Sugar and all of its manufacturing and production facilities in the Everglades with plans to dismantle the plant but whether or not this will happen remain to be seen.

My short but sweet Everglades tour was a success with a total of 10 crocodile sightings, two turtle sightings and countless bird sightings. I hope the powers that be protect this precious jewel for generations to come.

▲ *A baby crocodile rests safely on its mother's back, probably to avoid being eaten by other adult crocodiles.*

Crocodile Tales

The term crocodile refers to any species belonging to the family Crocodylidae but can also include alligators and caimans. These reptiles feed by grabbing and holding onto their prey with their huge jaws which can bite with more force than any other animal. The pressure of their bite is over 5,000 pounds per square inch compared to the 400 pounds per square inch bite of a great white shark. But because their jaws are opened by a very weak set of muscles, they can be subdued by taping or holding their jaws shut with large rubber bands cut from inner tubes.

These cold-blooded creatures can survive a long time without food but cannot survive if their body temperature drops below a certain level therefore they spend the majority of the day basking in the sun saving their hunting expeditions for the evening. They feed on fish, birds, mammals and occasionally smaller crocodiles. Yes, you read that right...they eat their own species. Life can be rough for a baby crocodile. It has a 99% chance of being eaten in its first year by large fish, monitor lizards, herons and adult crocodiles. But if they do make it into adulthood, crocodiles can survive up to 80 years.

Since they do not have sex chromosomes, the sex of their offspring is not determined genetically rather it is determined by temperature. If the eggs are incubated at an average temperature of around 31.6 degrees Celsius, male will be produced and if the temperature is higher, females will be produced.

Despite the fact they eat almost every living thing in sight, they do have a special relationship with a bird called the Egyptian Plover. They are known to allow these birds to enter their mouths and clean out the parasites. Since they cannot sweat, they often linger on the riverbanks with their mouths wide open to cool off.

Protected in many parts of the world, these reptiles are also farmed commercially as their hides are used to make leather goods and their meat is considered a delicacy. In fact, a crocodile purse can cost up to $15,000 which makes poaching them a lucrative business. A business that put them on the endangered list and has already wiped out many populations. Crocodile farms may be the thing that ends up saving them from total extinction.

The Conch Republic

By day two in Miami I knew I wouldn't be staying long. Unable to escape the annoying thump of the dance music emitting from the lounge of my hotel and my neighbour's room I knew I had to get out of dodge. I tried to find another affordable hotel but to no avail so I booked an all day tour of the Florida Keys followed by an early morning bus to Orlando – the land of budget hotel rooms and families where I hoped I could finally get some peace and quiet.

The Florida Keys are an archipelago of 1700 islands beginning at the tip of the Florida peninsula 15 miles south of Miami. Before 1910, they were only accessible by water but this all changed with the construction of Henry Flagler's Overseas Railway which extended from the mainland across to Key West.

In 1935, new bridges were being constructed to run a highway through the keys and that same year the Labor Day Hurricane destroyed the railway tracks killing over 400 people. The railway tracks were never rebuilt and the new highway replaced the railway as the main transportation route from Miami to Key West. The largest of the highway's bridges called the Seven Mile Bridge spans…yes you guessed it…7 miles.

A four-hour bus ride brought me to Key West, the southernmost island of the Florida Keys and the southernmost point in the United States. The 4 mile long and 2 mile wide island is only 90 miles from Cuba which explains the large Cuban population. Many had moved to the island to work in the 200 cigar factories which produced over 100 million cigars annually.

After the Cuban revolution of 1959, the island was flooded with Cuban refugees, many of whom came over on small overcrowded boats to escape the communist regime. The ferry and air service which once connected the two islands was cancelled and remains closed to this day but hopefully not for much longer.

As we approached the small city, our tour guide pointed out a number of flags representing the Conch Republic and told us how Key West got its nickname. Many of residents of Key West were immigrants from the Bahamas known as Conchs and in the 20th century, many of Key West's residents began to refer to themselves as Conchs. On April 23rd 1982, in response to a United States Border Patrol inspection point (looking for illegal drugs and immigrants) set up on the highway leading to Key West, the city mockingly declared itself independent of the United States in an effort to lift the roadblock which they claimed was hurting tourism in the area. They called themselves the Conch Republic and immediately declared war against the United States by breaking a loaf of stale bread over the head of a man dressed in a US naval uniform then quickly surrendered and applied for one billion dollars in foreign aid.

The event generated great publicity for their plight and as a result the roadblocks were lifted. As a result, tourism boomed spurring the city to celebrate their "independence every April 23rd.

The bus dropped us off in the middle of town where we were given 7 hours to explore on our own before returning to Miami. After getting my picture taken at the Southernmost Point Monument, I visited the nearby butterfly sanctuary before making my way to the public beach to enjoy some much needed down time.

I had visited Miami hoping to spend some time on the beach but found it too busy for my liking. The beaches of Key West however, where just right reminding me that the Universe always gives me what my heart desires just not in the way I expect it.

▶ *A monument erected by the city marks the symbolic southernmost point in the United States, however, the actual southernmost point is located just west of the landmark on US Navy land and cannot be visited by tourists.*

Top Ten Crazy Miami Facts

1. Rum-runners used the Everglades as a hiding place during Prohibition since there were not enough law enforcement officers to properly patrol it.
2. Miami is home to the Florida Marlins baseball team, the Miami Dolphins football team and the Miami Heat basketball team.
3. The Port of Miami is considered the cruise capital of the world with 3.5 million annual passengers.
4. The Art Deco District of Miami contains the world's largest collection of Art Deco architectures with over 800 buildings.
5. Miami is considered the Wreckreational Diving Capital of the World with over 50 wreck sites including ships, oil platforms, army tanks and a Boeing 727 jet sunk to provide artificial reefs.
6. In 2008, Miami was ranked as America's Cleanest City by Forbes Magazine because of its good air-quality, clean drinking water, clean streets, vast green spaces and city-wide recycling programs.
7. Miami and South Florida houses the largest concentration of international banks in the United States.
8. The second season of Jersey Shore (a program that I am embarrassed to admit I watch) was filmed at Miami Beach.
9. Miami Vice, a television series that ran from 1984 to 1989, was based in Miami. Recognized as one of the most influential television series of all time, the show, which incorporated the 1980's New Wave culture, was about a team of vice cops who combated drug trafficking and prostitution in the Miami area. Many episodes were filmed on location in South Beach and Miami Beach.
10. Pan American Airlines was founded in Key West to fly visitors to Cuba.

▲ *This was my seventies porn room, all that was missing was Ron Jeremy, a vibrating bed and a mirrored ceiling.*

What Did Things Cost?

Items Purchased	American Dollars
Flight from La Paz to Miami	$733.00
La Paz airport tax	$25.00
Entrance into the United States	Free
Single room in a nice hotel	$83.00
Boat ride through Everglades tour	$50.00
Roundtrip bus to Key West	$60.00
South Beach towel	$20.00
Lunch (hamburger)	$15.00
South Beach towel	$10.00

The Magic Kingdom

Six in the morning came fast and furious and despite the fact I was able to get to bed at 11pm; my earplugs were unable to quiet the dance music that oozed from every pore in the hotel. While I was able to block some of the sound I was not able to block the heavy baselines from the oversized subwoofers that vibrated through every bone in my body making me want to strangle the DJ with a patch cord and take a sledge hammer to his equipment.

When the bus pulled up in front of my hotel to take me to Disney World I was more than ready to leave Miami.

I should have visited the city in my twenties when I wanted nothing more than to party all night then sleep on a cold concrete floor with Iron Maiden screaming *Run to the Hills* in my ear. The older I get the higher maintenance I become.

If the conditions are not just right, I can't sleep and if I can't sleep I am miserable.

The agent who sold me the ticket promised the bus would drop me off at my hotel but the driver knew nothing of that arrangement and dropped me off at a gas station in Kissimmee, a town near Orlando and close to Disney World. What a strange name for a town.

Thankfully the bus driver called me a taxi and for an additional $40 I arrived at my hotel – the nicest one yet. Not only did it have a bathtub and was quiet, it also had an outdoor heated pool. Things were definitely looking up.

Letting Go

I ended the day at the Chinese buffet across from my hotel where my fortune cookie read, "Today is the day you will let it go. Your chance will come."

My heart jumped because I would love to be able to let go my attachment to certain outcomes. I get so attached to the way I want things to happen that I tend to get in the Universes way and mess things up. If I could just let go, I would save a ton of money on anti-depressants and anxiety medication.

Now I was attached to the idea of being detached. Was there any hope for me? I understand how things are supposed to work – I decide what I want, make it know to the Universe, let go of my attachment and the Universe delivers. However, I couldn't seem to detach from the things I wanted most. Hopefully the Universe was sending me help.

▲ *The Monorail connects the Magic Kingdom to Epcot and the transportation area.*

▲ *Photo courtesy of Wikipedia*

Walter Elias Disney

Born December 5th 1901, Died December 15th 1966

At an early age, Walter Disney, better known as Walt Disney, developed a passion for caricatures, cartoons and animation. He and his brother pooled their money together and set up a cartoon studio in Hollywood. In 1925 they hired a young woman named Lillian Bounds, who Disney married that same year. After suffering a miscarriage, Lillian gave birth to their first daughter Diane in 1933 and then the couple went on to adopt Sharon in 1936.

Working with fellow cartoonist Ubbe Iwerks, Disney created a character called Mickey Mouse in 1928 as a replacement for Iwerks earlier creation of Oswald the Lucky Rabbit. Disney's company created Oswald, for Charles Mintz of Universal Studios, who, thinking he had Disney over the barrel, told him he could continue the series only if he agreed to a budget cut and went on salary. Mintz had all of Disney's animators except Iwerks under contract and since he owned the rights could create the cartoon without Disney. Disney refused and walked away losing most of his animation staff. But he learned a valuable lesson: make sure to own all the rights to every character his company creates.

Mickey Mouse was inspired by a pet mouse he used to have on his farm. Originally called Mortimer Mouse, Walt's wife Lillian convinced him to change it to Mickey and the name stuck. Actor Mickey Rooney had met the cartoonist and was convinced the mouse was named after him. In 1932, Disney received a special Academy Award for the creation of Mickey whose series launched spin-offs for such supporting characters as Donald Duck, Goofy and Pluto.

In 1937, Disney Studios released its first full length Technicolor film Snow White and the Seven Dwarfs which, in 1997, was listed in the American Film Institute's list of the 100 greatest American films of all time. Despite running out of money during production of the film, Disney managed to complete the film with the help of a loan from the Bank of America. The film went on to become the most successful motion picture of 1938 earning over 8 million in its original theatrical release. This success allowed Disney Studios to set up a new campus in Burbank which opened on December 24th, 1939 where they created Pinocchio, Fantasia, Bambi, Alice in Wonderland and Peter Pan.

Disneyland officially opened on July 18th 1955 and today has a larger cumulative attendance than any other theme park in the world.

Disney died of lung cancer in 1966, the year before construction on Disney World began. His brother Roy put off his retirement so he could oversee construction of the park ensuring it was built to his brother's high standards.

Epcot

First thing the following morning I hopped the hotel's courtesy shuttle to Disneyworld, the world's largest and most-visited recreational resort, for a day of being a kid again. I often dreamed of visiting Disney World, now here I was. How cool is that?

Opened on October 1, 1971 with the Magic Kingdom theme park, it had since expanded to include four theme parks, two water parks and 23on-site themed resort hotels.

I decided to start at EPCOT which is an acronym for Experimental Prototype Community of Tomorrow. It was originally planned by Walt Disney to be a test bed for a model community housing 20,000 people. His vision included transportation by monorail and people movers with all automobile traffic kept underground. All houses would be rented out at modest rates and slum areas would not be allowed to develop. Everyone would be employed and retirement would not be permitted. New materials and systems would constantly be tested as this would be the showcase for ingenuity, imagination and American free enterprise.

Unfortunately Disney died before he was able to build it and the Walt Disney Company decided it did not want to run a city so it opened as a theme park instead.

I arrived first thing in the morning and, thinking that my best strategy would be to ride the most popular rides first went straight for Soarin, Test Track and Mission: SPACE.

Soarin' had me doing just that in a simulated hand glider over the State of California for almost 5 minutes where I was privy to a bird's eye view of the Golden Gate Bridge, Redwood forests, Napa Valley and Yosemite National Park.

Test track had me in a simulated excursion through the rigorous testing procedures used by General Motors to evaluate their vehicles. The ride ended with a thrilling speed trial on the track outside the building where we reached a top speed of 65 miles per hour on a 50 – degree banked curve. My heart was pounding after riding one of Disney's fastest rides ever built.

Mission Space is a motion simulator of a spacecraft with a crew of four on the first manned mission to Mars. Since the journey would take a few months, we were put into hyper sleep. Also called suspended animation, this is where involuntary bodily functions such as breathing and heartbeat are slowed down to a point where they can only be detected by artificial means. Extreme cold can be used to do this, a process which led to the development of cryonics.

▲ *Spaceship earth is EPCOT's icon.*

This method uses liquid nitrogen to preserve organisms for extended periods until they are re-animated. Laina Beasley is familiar with this process as she spent 13 years as a frozen embryo before being implanted into her mother's womb.

After the rides, I was hungry so I made my way to the World Showcase which contains pavilions from eleven countries including Mexico, Norway, China, Germany, Italy, United States, Japan, Morocco, France, United Kingdom and my country: Canada. Each pavilion's shops and restaurants are staffed by citizens of these countries. Unlike the Magic Kingdom, guests can enjoy an alcoholic beverage with their meal. The food selection is also the largest of all the parks. The others offered little variety save for a hamburger, pizzas, french-fries and other deep-fried delicacies capable of adding 20 pounds to the butt almost overnight.

I arrived at 9am when the park opened and by 2pm I had seen everything I wanted to see, however my shuttle did not arrive until 8:45 pm so I spent an extra $50 to upgrade my ticket to a park hopper. The standard tickets only allowed me to visit one park per day.

Animal Kingdom

I spent the rest of the day at Animal Kingdom, the fourth park built at the Disney World Resort, which is entirely themed around animal conservation – a philosophy held dear by Walt Disney himself.

In fact, the centerpiece and icon of the park is The Tree of Life, a 14-story 50-foot wide tree with 325 animals carved into its bark. As well, they are accredited by the Association of Zoos and Aquariums, having exceeded the standards in education, conservation and research. The park consists of seven themed areas: Oasis, Discovery Island, Camp Minnie-Mickey, Africa, Rafiki's Planet Watch, Asia and DinoLand USA.

I started my visit in Asia on their most popular ride: Expedition Everest, a rollercoaster train ride through the Himalayas to the base of Mount Everest where I encountered a Yeti. Also known as an Abominable Snowman, the Yeti is an ape-like creature believed to inhabit the Himalayan region. The Yeti had torn up the tracks forcing the train to come to a halt, roll backwards into a cave and then proceed down the mountain on a different route.

To help publicize the rides opening on April 7th 2006, Disney, Discovery Networks and Conservation International conducted expeditions to the real Mount Everest to conduct scientific and cultural research in the remote areas where the legend of the Yeti exists. Three documentaries were produced and broadcast on the Discovery Channel.

▲ *Expedition Everest is a rollercoaster that goes forwards and backwards.*

Interesting Fact:

The flamingo island in the Kilimanjaro Safari is a huge Hidden Mickey.

I completed my tour through the Asia section of the park with a trek in the Maharajah Jungle where I encountered a Komodo dragon, a Bengal Tiger, some snakes and some Rodrigues fruit bats – the largest bats in the world. Also called megabats and flying foxes, these bats can attain a wingspan of almost 5 feet and weigh up to 2.2 pounds. They looked like miniature Count Dracula's.

Next I headed over to DinoLand USA to DINOSAUR – a ride in a Time Rover on a turbulent journey through time to the Cretaceous era. There I encountered a number of dinosaurs including a styracosauraus, alioramus, parasaurolophus, raptor, saltasaurus, and a flying pterodactyl. During our ride we experienced a meteor shower that some claim caused the dinosaurs to become extinct. Thankfully we were able to reach the time tunnel and return to the present before getting hit by a meteor or eaten by a dinosaur.

After a brief stop at Discovery Island to check out the Tree of Life, I walked over to Africa and joined a Kilimanjaro Safari through the Harambe Wildlife Reserve where I spotted some elephants, giraffes, zebras, antelope, crocodiles, monkeys, cheetahs, wildebeests, warthogs and even a huge rhino. Our two-week tour was cut short when the reserve warden observed some poachers while doing a routine flight over the reserve. He called on us to help stop them.

Thankfully the poachers were caught and this story had a happy ending but this doesn't always happen in the real world where poachers who illegally kill animals, such as elephants for their ivory tusks, have threatened many species to the point of near extinction.

My visit ended with a stop at the Oasis at the entrance of the park where I encountered a flock of pink spoonbills – a large bird that looks like a pink flamingo with a large flat bill.

By then it was time to catch a bus back to the parking area to board my 8:45 pm shuttle to the hotel and rest up for part two of my Disney World adventure.

Hollywood Studios

I began my second day at Hollywood Studios, the third park built at the resort. Inspired by the 1930's and 40's Hollywood heyday, the park opened on May 1st 1989. A large sorcerer's hat similar to the magical hat worn by Mickey in Fantasia greets guests as they enter the park. There are six themed areas to visit which include Hollywood Boulevard, Echo Lake, Streets of America, Animation Courtyard, Pixar Place and Sunset Boulevard.

Using my "visit the biggest attraction first strategy" I bee-lined it to The Twilight Zone Tower of Terror on Sunset Boulevard to beat the line. Why? I have no idea. I hate rides that drop. More than once I have awakened in the middle of the night traumatized after having another falling from the sky nightmare. I knew this ride involved dropping because my friend Carolyn rode it when she was in Disneyland. But like a complete idiot I stood in line and got on.

▲ *The Hollywood Tower Hotel is less than 200 feet tall because the law requires any structure 200 feet and taller to have a fixed red light beacon on it which Imagineers thought would take away from the attraction.*

Taking place in the fictional Hollywood Tower Hotel (inspired by the real Hollywood Tower – an apartment building built in Hollywood in 1929 that was a popular residence for people in the entertainment industry) the story goes that the hotel was struck by lightning in 1939 and an elevator cart full of passengers were transported into the Twilight Zone. Do you remember the Twilight Zone? It was a television series first run from 1959 to 1964 then revived between 1985-1989 and then again from 2002 to 2003. Each episode was a mixture of fantasy, science fiction, suspense and horror that had families sitting on the edge of their couches.

The first part was rather enjoyable; we entered an elevator, sat down and ascended to the next level where a set of doors opened to reveal a dimly-lit corridor with a single window at the end. While a violent thunderstorm raged outside, the ghostly images of five doomed guest appeared then vanished in a burst of electricity. The corridor then blackened and turned into a star-filled sky before the elevator door closed and we ascended to the next floor. The doors opened to reveal another star field which we passed through on our way to another elevator shaft beyond the fifth dimension.

This is where the terror part came in. Rather than a simple gravity drop, the elevator was mechanically pulled downwards causing me to rise out of my seat and nearly pee my pants. Thankfully I was held in by a seatbelt. And, as if one heart-stopping drop was not enough, it continued to rise and drop at different intervals making me wonder if the torture would ever end. The slogan for the ride is "Never the Same Fear Twice" because the ride changes every time. When riders reach the drop shaft, a computer randomly chooses one of four drop profiles each containing one fake drop to startle guests and one complete drop of the entire tower.

Having terrified myself enough for one day, my next stop was Indiana Jones Epic Stunt Spectacular show. After having some members of the audience cast as extras, we got to watch Indiana Jones dodge wooden spikes that jutted out of the floor and a number of other obstacles and explosions in his effort to obtain the golden idol. The scene ended with him being chased by a 12-foot rolling boulder, which he of course barely escaped.

The audience extras were then brought in while the stage transformed from an ancient temple to the streets of Cairo where a number of fight scenes ensued. The grand finale took place in a military camp where Indiana attempted to steal a plane and make his escape amongst plenty of gun fire and explosions. My heart pounded the entire time as though I was trying to escape the bad guys.

After a Studio Backlot Tour where I learned how some of the most spectacular movie special effects are made, I caught the Muppet 4-D movie before having the American Idol Experience.

Contestants who auditioned earlier in the day are chosen to compete in the show. After watching the acts perform, the audience votes for their favourite contestant using the interactive keyboards at their seats. The coolest part is that the best singer of the day receives a Dream Ticket which gives them the opportunity, to bypass the line and sing in front of a real American Idol representative at a regional audition for a chance at being the next American Idol!

Dream Ticket winners who do not meet the eligibility requirements for the television show are allowed to transfer the ticket to someone who does or wait until they do meet the requirements.

▲ *The Sorcerer's Hat is the icon of Disney's Hollywood Studios.*

▲ *The American Idol Experience gives you the experience of attending a live taping of the show.*

Dream ticket winner Aaron Kelly finished fifth in the 2010 season of the show.

As I was walking out of the studio after the show, a lady approached asking me if I wanted to audition. Me...audition for American Idol? OF COURSE I WANTED TO AUDITION FOR AMERICAN IDOL! If was eligible I would have auditioned for the real show but since I am not, this might be my only chance to share my talent with the world. I could finally achieve the superstardom I know I am capable of...just kidding. In truth it was a slow day at the park and the three singers who had just performed were not that great so I knew they were scraping the bottom of the barrel. That was right around my vocal range.

I was ushered into the audition room area and, without having to wait in line, went right into an office for my audition.

After answering the interview questions, I broke into my best rendition of; yes you guessed it, Folsom Prison by the great Johnny Cash. The interviewer was pleased to inform me that I was in fact in tune but regretted to inform me that they were looking for pop/rock singers and I did not fall under this category. While I didn't make it on stage, I did get a big shiny button with my name on it that said I auditioned for American Idol. You can't beat that!

Magic Kingdom

I saved the best for last and ended my day at the Magic Kingdom. One of the busiest rides was Space Mountain which was opened in 1974 and then refurbished in 2009. The new, improved ride cost a whopping $12.3 million and in my opinion was worth every penny.

The standby line-up was 70 minutes long so I opted to get a fastpass. Available free of charge to all park guests, this system is a virtual queuing system introduced in 1999. I placed my park pass into the fastpass machine and it gave me a ticket with both a time when I could return to the ride and get into the much faster fasspass line as well as the time when I could obtain another fasspass ticket.

A few hours later I returned to the ride and within 15 minutes was hoping into one of the six-person rockets and heading through a dark tunnel to a field of stars and up a hill. When we reached the top we raced through a series of sharp turns, climbs and steep drops all in the cover of darkness which added that extra scary element to the ride. After passing through a red swirling wormhole we hit the final brake run – my heart was racing.

My favourite ride in Disneyland is the Haunted House so of course I had to check out the one in Disney World. We were ushered to the "dead center" of the octagonal portrait gallery where the walls began to stretch revealing how each person in the portraits met their untimely end before the lights went out and the sound of thunder filled the room. A light on the ceiling lit up to reveal our ghost host hanging from a noose at the top of the cupola before a wall mysteriously opened leading us deeper into the mansion. We then entered a loading area where we were ushered into "Doom Buggies" which took us to the heart of the mansion to see the ghosts. We entered a ballroom with a number of ghosts dancing and I spotted my first Hidden Mickey. Three plates on the table were placed in such a way to resemble the world's favourite mouse.

The ride ended with a ghost following me home and a warning that it would remain with me until the day I returned to the mansion. I am not sure when I will be able to return to the mansion so I guess I will be stuck with my own personal ghost indefinitely. I hope it's a friendly one like Casper.

By 8pm everyone had filled the sidewalks along Main Street USA to get the best view of the fireworks show that takes place every night above Cinderella's Castle – the icon for the Magic Kingdom. My eyes welled up with tears as I watched the sky fill up with fireworks to sound of the Disney classic When You Wish upon a Star.

When you wish upon a star
Makes no difference who you are
Anything your heart desires
Will come to you
If your heart is in your dream
No request is too extreme

When you wish upon a star
As dreamers do
Fate is kind
She brings to those who love
The sweet fulfillment of
Their secret longing
Like a bolt out of the blue
Fate steps in and sees you through
When you wish upon a star
Your dreams come true

It was this song that taught me how to wish for things as I was growing up.

The simple act of making a wish and believing it will come true has brought so many miracles into my life but somewhere along the way, I quit believing that my big wishes would come true and I gave up hope. I started to feel hope return to my body as I realized my wish of backpacking through South America had come true. When I saw my first star that night I placed a few more wishes confident they would come true as well.

Used Pass Warning

There are ticket vendors all over Orlando that sell passes to Disney World and some of the shadier ones even offer to buy your pass back if you have days left on it offering to pay up to $75. While it is not illegal to sell your pass it is illegal to use someone else's pass.

Disney parks have a fingerprint scanner at the entry to the parks to prevent this but people are still able to buck the system. To save yourself any headache, don't buy a used pass and to save yourself from bad karma, don't sell your used pass.

▲ *Every night at 8pm, there was a fireworks show.*

▲ *The train station greets guests at the entrance to the Magic Kingdom.*

Disney *Fast* Facts

- ✓ *Walt Disney himself was the original voice of Mickey Mouse*
- ✓ *During World War II, the US Army contracted most of Disney Studio's to create training and instructional films for the military as well as short films to boost morale on the home front.*
- ✓ *During the Cold War, Walt Disney accused the Screen Actors Guild of being a Communist Front claiming that their 1941 strike was part of their ploy to gain influence in Hollywood.*
- ✓ *Disney got his idea to build a theme park after visiting Children's Failyland in Oakland, California.*
- ✓ *The people responsible for the creation and construction of Disney's theme parks are called imagineers because they are a blend of imagination and engineering.*
- ✓ *Hidden Mickey's are any representation of Mickey Mouse inserted subtly throughout Disney Properties. For example, if you look at the center of the drain lids on the streets in Disneyworld there are three circles that represent Mickey.*
- ✓ *Walt Disney designed and built a miniature live steam railroad in his backyard that included a 90-foot tunnel underneath his wife's flower garden.*
- ✓ *Walt Disney's ashes reside at the Forest Lawn Memorial Park in Glendale, California.*
- ✓ *Walt Disney holds the record for the most number of Academy Award nominations at 59. He was awarded 22 and also earned 4 honorary Oscars including one for the creation of Mickey Mouse.*
- ✓ *During his 1959 visit to the United States, Soviet Premier Nikita Khrushchev put in a request to visit Disneyland but was denied because of security concerns due to the tension of the Cold War.*
- ✓ *The Shah of Iran visited Disneyland in the early 1960's and was videotaped riding the Matterhorn with Walt Disney. The video is posted on YouTube.*
- ✓ *Disneyland Parks are also located in Hong Kong, Paris and Tokyo with a Shanghai one opening in 2014.*
- ✓ *Expedition Everest in Animal Kingdom was listed in the 2011 Guinness Book of World Records as the most expensive rollercoaster in the world at a construction cost of $100 million.*

Islands of Adventure

When I woke up the next morning I checked the weather in Kamloops and discovered it was snowing. That made me even happier to be spending another sunny day in Florida. As I sat in the hotel's lobby sipping on coffee I noticed a brochure for Universal Studios and decided to make that my mission for the day.

I had watched the opening of the Wizarding World of Harry Potter on June 18, 2010 and knew I wanted to visit one day but had no idea that day would come so soon.

The Universal Orlando resort is comprised of three sections: Universal Studios, Islands of Adventure – both theme parks and Universal CityWalk – the place to go for evening entertainment. With only one day to spend at the resort, I bought a two-park pass and started my day at the Islands of Adventure. Opened in 1999, the park consists of seven islands: Port of Entry, Marvel Super Hero Island, Toon Lagoon, Jurassic Park, The Lost Continent, Seuss Landing and The Wizarding World of Harry Potter. Knowing that Hogwarts Castle would be the top attraction, I made my way there first to fight the crowds and check out Harry Potter and the Forbidden Journey – their signature ride.

To prevent over-overcrowding (I use the word over twice because it was already overcrowded) they issued passes for people to return at later times. I was fortunate enough to make it in right away and join the swarm of muggles (people without magical powers) winding their way through Hogsmeade Village, the only settlement in Great Britain inhabited solely by magical beings. It was founded by a medieval wizard who fled Scotland to avoid persecution by muggles.

From there I bee-lined it to Hogwarts Castle – the boarding school for witches and wizards that Harry Potter attended. Fighting my way through all the muggles to get to the castle was the easy part, finding an empty locker and figuring out how to get into it so I could store my backpack before getting on the ride was PFM: Pure Frickin Magic!

Fortunately I managed to crack the code and store my stuff before jumping into the singles line. I was almost at the loading station when I found out the ride was experiencing technical difficulties. D'oh! Why does the Universe insist on putting so many roadblocks between me and the things I want most? As usual, the second I thought all hope was lost and I accepted the fact I wouldn't be getting on the ride, the Universe says, "Just kidding, hop on".

▲ *The Forbidden Journey ride is located inside Hogwart's Castle.*

▲ *The sheer size of Poseidon's Temple is impressive.*

I was about to leave and check out some of the other rides when suddenly everyone in the line started to cheer. The technicians had fixed the ride and within 10 minutes I was getting loaded onto an enchanted bench (a robotic arm mounted to a track) and being doused with floo powered before flying into the Astronomy Tower. Next we followed Harry Potter and Ron Weasly in a Quidditch match before getting chased by Hagrid's pet dragon then descending into the Forbidden Forest.

Thankfully Hermione was able help us get back to the castle and we were able to avoid the Whomping Willow that was trying to hit us. We returned to the Quidditch pitch only to discover that some Dementors had arrived to suck out our souls. We managed to escape them unscathed and make it to the Room of Requirement where we landed.

I passed on riding the Flight of the Hippogriff (a family-friendly rollercoaster) and the Dragon Challenge (two rollercoaster's that intertwine, twist, loop and nearly collide as they chase each other through the sky) because there was a lot of park left to see and I only had one day.

Instead I made my way to the Lost Continent where I stumbled upon a huge statue of Poseidon, the god of the sea. Behind the ruins was Poseidon's Fury, a tour of his enormous temple where his devotees once worshipped. Our tour was interrupted when we got locked into the temple and forced to go deeper into its chambers where we went through a water vortex and accidentally awakened the spirit of Lord Darkenon. Thankfully our guide returned Poseidon's trident to him so he could battle Darkenon. After a series of 25-

foot exploding fireballs and 350,000 gallons of exploding water Poseidon won the battle and we were free to leave. Thank God because there were no seats in the temple and my legs were getting tired

Next I visited Seuss Landing where I rode a couch through the Cat in the Hat, a ride based on one of my favorite children's books. When I walked through the large red and white hat I entered the front yard of a house where I saw Sally and her brother staring out a window looking bored. I hopped aboard a couch and entered the house just in time to see their mother leave to go shopping. Then the Cat in the Hat entered the house to relieve the kids of their boredom and all hell broke loose. He invited Thing One and Thing Two to run amuck turning the house upside down. They even attempted to throw a piano at us. Thankfully the fish saw the mother returning and the cat was able to use his Thing-A-Majig to clean up the mess so we didn't get caught.

I ended my visit at Jurassic Park where I went on the River Adventure. Based on Steven Spielberg's epic film adapted from Michael Crichton's novel Jurassic Park, this ride had me on a raft floating through Jurassic Park where I encountered a number of dinosaurs and prehistoric creatures. One of the dinosaurs pushed the raft off course and we ended up in the Raptor Containment area where we were instructed to stay in the boat. The electric fence had been ripped apart and was shooting out sparks. Something had gone terribly wrong.

We floated past by a crashed boat where two creatures were fighting over a torn shirt belonging to whoever had been riding it...not a good sign. My skin started to crawl when I noticed the silhouette of a raptor. For those who don't know what a raptor is, it's a scary predatory dinosaur and it was looking for us.

To make matters worse, we took another sudden turn right into a T-Rex whose jaws were wide opened and waiting for us. He would have eaten us had we not plunged down a heart-stopping 85-foot waterfall into a lagoon and back to safety.

Universal Studios Florida

With only half a day left I raced over to Universal Studios to check it out. Opened in 1990 with a movie and television theme, the park is divided into six sections: Production Central, New York, San Francisco/Amity, World Expo, Woody Woodpecker's Kidzone and Hollywood.

▲ *The entrance to the Cat in the Hat ride is a large red and white hat.*

▲ *Visitors can pose for a picture inside the mouth of Jaws, Universal Studio's deadliest shark.*

Unlike Universal Studios Hollywood, a working film and television studio turned tourist attraction and theme park, Universal Studios Florida was designed right from the start to be a theme park and studio.

Being a huge fan of ancient Egypt, I of course went straight for the Revenge of the Mummy in New York. Based on the Mummy series of adventure films, this enclosed steel rollercoaster is a psychological thrill ride. Lasting nearly three minutes and reaching a top speed of 72 kilometres per hour the 670 meters of tracks features 80 degree banked turns and a 50 degree angle of descent. After I entered the Museum of Antiquities, I came upon a 1940's archaeological dig site inside an Egyptian tomb and hopped aboard a mine car.

We entered another room inside the tomb of Imhotep where we were warned to leave by a partly mummified man. Before he finished his warning, Imhotep came out of his sarcophagus and sucked out the man's soul then threatened to sucks ours as well claiming that "With your souls I shall rule for all eternity". The car then took us on a wild ride that included spinning around 180 degrees, ascending a hill and launching at top speed through the dark completely scaring the crap out of me. I loved it!

Next door to the Mummy was an attraction called Disaster which looked interesting so I decided to check it out. We were ushered into a casting room and told that we were going to be making a major motion picture starring us. How cool is that? When casting was finished we were taken into a screening room where a lifelike Frank Kincaid reveals to us the formula for a hit disaster movie and asks for our help in creating his latest blockbuster Mutha Nature about an environmental disaster.

We were then ushered onto another sound stage where those who were cast in the starring roles filmed their sequences before boarding a subway and heading to Embarcadero Station where the scene started. Small screens aboard the train gave us directions on how to act while we endured a massive earthquake. The lights in the station started to flicker as the train began to shake violently.

Suddenly a crack formed on the platform and a section of the roof collapsed. As if that wasn't scary enough, a gasoline truck fell through the ceiling and burst into flames just before another subway train derailed and raced towards us while a flash flood gushed down the stairs and into the station.

When the scene was over, and we were on our way back to the West Oakland Station, the trailer for Muther Nature was played over the screens. The show was about park ranger Dwayne Johnson who saves lives during a series of ecological disasters such as earthquakes, floods and hurricanes. The scenes we shot were incorporated into the trailer for the grand finale giving us all a good laugh before we got off.

Satisfied with my performance in the movie, I exited the studio and came across a huge shark with its jaws opened hanging from a rope so I went over to investigate. I found myself on the small island of Amity where I took a leisurely boat tour that turned out to be anything but. Lurking in the calm waters was a great white shark hunting for tasty tourists.

The attraction is based on the 1975 thriller film *Jaws* directed by Steven Spielberg about a police chief who tries to protect swimmers from a man eating great white shark by closing the beach only to have his decision overturned by city council who doesn't want to lose the tourist income. The movie went on to become the father of the summer blockbuster film paving the way for *The Omen* and *Star Wars*. Shot in Martha's Vineyard in Massachusetts with the help of three mechanical sharks, the popularity of the film has inspired two video games, two theme park rides in Universal Studios Florida and Japan, as well as two musicals: JAWS the Musical and Giant Killer Shark: The Musical.

Thankfully, unlike the tourists in the film, we were able to escape the vicious shark with all or our limbs intact

When I noticed the Simpsons Ride I raced over to check it out. The Simpsons have been one of my favorite shows since debuting on December 17th 1989. It began its 22nd season in 2010 and has broadcast over 500 episodes surpassing Gunsmoke as the longest running American primetime entertainment series. It was Homer who introduced the catchphrase "D'oh!" into the English language.

In 2008, Universal Studios opened up a simulator ride based on the animated series which replaced the Back to the Future Ride at both the Florida and California locations. Using computer generated 3D animation, the ride uses state of the art technology to bring visitors on a 6-minute tour of Krustyland – a theme park opened by Krusty the Clown. Unfortunately Sideshow Bob, Krusty's former sidekick, had escaped from prison and was seeking revenge on Krusty and the Simpson family.

This ride is not recommended for those who get motion sickness like me.

▲ *The Simpsons ride replaced the Back to the Future ride in 2008.*

Travel Tip

If you are planning to include Universal Studios and SeaWorld into your Orlando vacation, I recommend choosing a hotel on International Drive as they have a trolley that runs regularly along the drive to shuttle visitors from their hotels to all the attractions and shopping areas. Most of the hotels also offer free shuttles to Disney World.

Needless to say, I was happy when we escaped Krusty and exited into the Kwik-E-Mart, After I convinced my stomach not to hurl, I made my way to Shrek 4-D where I was able to relax in an air-conditioned theatre with a pair of 3-D glasses.

Unbeknownst to me, the spirit of Lord Farquaad returned from the dead shortly after the first film to kidnap Princess Fiona leaving it up to Shrek and Donkey to save her. We followed their journey through storybook land where, with the help of a fire-breathing dragon, they were able to save the princess and send Farquaad back to the underworld.

Shrek 4D was almost as good as the original film which was released in 2001 and featured the voices of such famous actors as Mike Myers, Eddie Murphy and Cameron Diaz. Shrek. The film helped to establish Dreamworks as a prime competitor to Pixar in the field of feature film animation and won the first ever Academy Award for Best Animated Feature beating out Monsters, Inc. and Jimmy Neutron: Boy Genius.

▲ *Universal's logo, a globe, greats guests at the entrance to the theme park.*

The story of the ogre named Shrek and his friend (a talking donkey) inspired a series of Shrek movies including Shrek 2, Shrek the Third and Shrek Forever After as well as a Christmas special called Shrek the Halls and a Halloween special called Scared Shrekless.

Fast Facts

- ✓ In 2006, after 80 years, NBC Universal sold all of the Disney-produced Oswald cartoons back to Disney in exchange for the release of sports caster Al Michaels from his contract so he could works on NBC's Sunday night NFL football package.
- ✓ In 2008 a fire broke out in the back lot of Universal's California studio destroying 40-50 thousand archived digital video and film copies of Universal's movies and television shows dating back to the 1920's including such favourites as Law & Order, The Office and Miami Vice

History of Universal Studios

Universal Studios, one of the oldest American movie studios still in continuous production, was partially founded by German immigrant Carl Laemmle. Regarded as one of the most important early film pioneers, Laemmle produced or was somehow involved in over 400 films. Laemmle moved to America in 1884 where he began buying nickelodeons (an early form of movie theatre). Unhappy with having to pay fees for the movies they showed, he and other Nickelodeon owners teamed up to produce their own motion pictures. In 1909 he founded the Independent Moving Pictures Company in New York City and in New Jersey which broke with industry tradition by giving billing and screen credits to performers thus leading to the creation of the star system in Hollywood, where movie stars are used to help market films.

In 1912, he merged with some smaller companies to form the Universal Film Manufacturing Company of which he was the president and primary figure. He later bought out his partners who went on to open the Keystone Film Company and in 1925 his company was incorporated into Universal Pictures Company. In an act of nepotism Laemmle's son Carl, Jr. became head of Universal Pictures in 1928 as a 21st birthday present, not a surprise since the company had 70 of their relatives on the payroll at one time.

In fact not only did Laemmle help out family members, the German-Jewish immigrant also financially supported and sponsored hundreds of Jews from his hometown to emigrate from Nazi Germany into the United States saving them from almost certain death in the Holocaust.

Carl Jr. helped to bring Universal up to date by building and purchasing theatres, converting the studio to sound production and creating a niche for the studio in producing monster movies such as Frankenstein, Dracula, The Mummy and The Invisible Man. In fact, the 1931 poster for Frankenstein is considered the most valuable movie poster of all time with only one copy known to exist.

Unfortunately the Laemmle's forays into the world of high-quality production films spelled the end for them at Universal. During the filming of Show Boat, considered one of the greatest musical films of all time, Universal was forced to seek a production loan of $750,000, the first in its 26-year history. When Standard called in the loan, which was based on the Laemmles controlling interest in the company, the studio couldn't pay and Standard foreclosed the loan and seized control of the company. Show Boat, which ran $300,000 over budget, turned out to be a huge financial success for the company but unfortunately the windfall came too late for the Laemmles who, in 1936, were unceremoniously removed from the company they so lovingly built.

Unlike Disneyland, the Universal Studios theme park did not open as a theme park rather it evolved from the studio tours which were offered as early as the silent film days when the tour included a chance to buy fresh produce from the working farm that was still part of Universal City. In 1962, the Music Corporation of America took over Universal Pictures and revamped the studio tour to increase profits. Visitors were brought through a series of dressing rooms, were able to take a peek at an actual production as well as be entertained by staged events. Over the years the tour evolved into a full blown theme park with stunt demonstrations, high-tech rides and plenty of quality entertainment.

▲ *The original Shamu died in the 70's but her name has been passed down to other killer whales at SeaWorld.*

SeaWorld

I hadn't planned to visit SeaWorld but so many people told me how much they loved it I figured it must be worth seeing. I am so glad I did. With a zoological and marine-life theme, the park is divided into four sections: Key West, Shamu's Happy Hordor and The Waterfront. I got there just in time to catch the first Shamu show and that was how I started my day.

Shamu was the fourth killer whale ever captured and the first to survive over 13 months in captivity.

Most people know her as the star of the killer whale show at San Diego's SeaWorld in the 1960's. Captured by Ted Griffin in Puget Sound, Seattle in 1965, she was intended as a companion for Namu, a killer whale at Griffin's public aquarium, hence the name Shamu (She-Namu).

However, the two did not get along so Ted sold her to SeaWorld. Her career as a performing whale was cut short after an incident during a publicity event where she grabbed the leg of a SeaWorld employee who was riding her and refused to let go. She died in 1971, from an unspecified infection but her name continued to be used for the killer whale shows.

There is always a risk of injury and death when working with large animals in captivity and this was illustrated on February 24th 2010 when experienced 40-year-old trainer Dawn Brancheau's arm was grabbed by a male killer whale during a "Dine with Shamu" show at Orlando's SeaWord. The giant fish thrashed her about while swimming rapidly around the pool until she drowned.

Fortunately while I was visiting, the whales were on their best behaviour and no one died during their performance.

Too scared to ride Manta (the huge rollercoaster opened in 2009 that has people flying upside-down over a pond) I opted instead to check out Journey to Atlantis – the first rollercoaster – boat ride I have ever encountered. After hopping onto an eight passenger boat, we floated through Atlantis enjoying the underwater city until we were expelled and send up two different lifts before dropping down a steep canal.

▲ *A sea lion and his cast mate entertain the crowd in "Clyde and Seamore Take Pirate Island".*

We then floated along the river until we reached another hill which we were pulled up. I though the ride ended at the top of the next hill but much to my surprise it brought us to a roller coaster which sped us to the exit. Having determined it was my favourite ride ever, I immediately went for a second turn.

▲ *Manta, at SeaWorld in Orlando, is the second-longest, tallest and fastest rollercoaster in the World next to Tatsu at Six Flags Magic Mountain in Valencia, California.*

I spent the next few hours checking out all the animal exhibits including Penguin Encounter, Shark Encounter, Pacific Point Encounter, Dolphin Cove, Turtle Point, Manatee Rescue, Stingray Lagoon, Flamingo Lagoon and the Wild Arctic.

Penguin Encounter is where they house their penguins and puffins in huge indoor habitats. The large glass window allows visitors to see the birds both on the land and swimming underwater. Shark Encounter features an underwater tunnel through which guests ride a people mover while observing a huge array of sharks, rays and venomous fish.

Pacific Point Preserve is where the park houses their sea lion population while Dolphin Cove is where visitors can feed and touch the Bottlenose Dolphins. Rescued sea turtles live peacefully in Turtle Point which provides them with a shallow pool and beach for accommodations and rescued manatee's, along with some alligators share accommodations at Manatee Rescue.

Visitors can touch a stingray at Stingray Lagoon then watch pink Caribbean flamingos bathe in the Flamingo Pond. Those visiting Wild Arctic are treated to a motion-simulated helicopter journey to the arctic where they encounter polar bears, beluga whales and walruses.

While I would have loved to watch all the shows at SeaWorld which include the killer whale show, dolphin show, sea lion show, waterskiing show, acrobatic show and various other animal acts, I didn't have the time so I chose two. First I went to the Sea Lion show to watch *Clyde and Seamore Take Pirate Island.* Clyde and Seamore, a pair of California sea lions, entertained the crowd with such antics as ripping down a slide, imitating their human cast mates and waving to the crowd. These funny animal actors had me busting a gut giving me a whole new appreciation for sea lions.

I ended my day at the dolphin show. I have seen a few dolphin shows in my time and they never cease to entertain me. How the heck they got those amazing creatures to all jump out of the water in a line (I counted seven) at the same time is a mystery.

If that wasn't amazing enough, the grand finale also included a few of the dolphins doing somersaults in the air.

By the end of the day I was wishing I had an extra day to spend at SeaWorld's other park Discovery Cove where I could swim with dolphins and interact with an assortment of tropical birds, fish and other creatures.

▲ *Journey to Atlantis is the best ride ever!*

▲ *The dolphin show is one of the major attractions at SeaWorld.*

Sea World *Fast* Facts

- ✓ *There are currently three SeaWorld parks located in San Diego, Orlando and San Antonio and in 2008 plans were announced to open a fourth SeaWorld Park in Dubai.*
- ✓ *SeaWorld was founded in 1964 by UCLA graduates, Milton C. Shedd, Ken Norris, David Demott and George Millay who had the idea to construct an underwater restaurant then when their plans were deemed unfeasible for construction purposes opened a marine zoological park instead.*
- ✓ *The first SeaWorld was opened in San Diego with an investment of $1.5 million, 45 employees, several dolphins, sea lions and two seawater aquariums*
- ✓ *The largest of the parks is the one in San Antonio.*
- ✓ *The second SeaWorld was opened in Ohio in 1970 but sold to Six Flags Ohio in 2001.*
- ✓ *Organizations such as the World Society for the Protection of Animals and the Whale and Dolphin Conservation Society campaign against the captivity of dolphins and killer whales arguing their lives are cut short when they are in captivity.*
- ✓ *At San Diego SeaWorld in2006, an orca held a trainer below the surface by the foot but the 39-year old managed to escape.*
- ✓ *SeaWorld has recently created the SeaWorld & Busch Gardens Conservatory Fund – a non-profit charitable foundation dedicated to supporting wildlife preservation, research, education and animal rescue. Visitors to the park are given the opportunity to donate to the fund which makes bi-annual grants to conservation groups around the world.*
- ✓ *It was the success of Walt Disney World in Orlando that encouraged SeaWorld to open a park in that location and it has since thrived.*
- ✓ *Southwest Airlines has three Boeing 737 aircraft painted to look like the famous killer whale Shamu as an advertisement for SeaWorld.*

Top Ten Crazy Orlando Facts

1. Orlando is home to the world's biggest McDonalds which boasts a play area with 25,000 feet of twisting tubes as well as slides and games for kids of all ages. For adults, the Bistro Gourmet offers unique cuisine ranging from pasta to sandwiches and desserts.
2. Popular boy bands Backstreet Boys, NSync, and O-Town all got their start in Orlando before becoming nationwide and international successes.
3. The popular alternative band Matchbox Twenty is from Orlando.
4. In 2009, Orlando had the honor of being the most visited city in America thanks to attractions such as Disney World, Sea World and Universal Studios.
5. The University of Central Florida, located in Orlando, has the highest student enrollment in Florida and the 2nd largest in the United States.
6. Orlando was chosen as the location for Disney World over Miami and Tampa because it was inland and was less threatened by hurricanes than the two coastal cities.
7. Many people visit Orlando during the Daytona 500, a 500-mile long NASCAR Sprint Cup Series race held annually at the Daytona International Speedway in Daytona Beach, a short drive from Orlando. In fact, the race was taking place during my visit.
8. Orlando has the largest number of hotels in America and the second largest number of hotel rooms after Las Vegas.
9. Orlando is known as "Hollywood East" due to the large number of movie studios in the area. In fact, it is the home base for the Florida Film Festival that takes place every April at locations throughout Central Florida.
10. Many major motion pictures such as My Girl, The Waterboy, Lethal Weapon 3, Monster and Jaws 3 were filmed in Orlando.

▲ *Main Street America was built to resemble a typical main street in any American city.*

▲ *The Wizarding World of Harry Potter is by far the most popular area of Universal Orlando Resort.*

What Did Things Cost?

Items Purchased	American Dollars
Shuttle from Miami to Orlando (hotel to Kissimmee)	$40.00
Taxi from bus to hotel	$40.00
Single room in Continental Plaza hotel	$45.00
Single room in Howard Johnson	$27.00
Four-day park pass	$218.00
Upgrade so I can visit more than one park in a day	$57.00
Universal Studios and Adventure Island + Express Pass	$173.00
Cab from Continental to Howard Johnson	$16.00
Mickey Mouse ice cream sandwich	$3.50
Lunch at any of the theme parks	$12.00
Disney World Souvenir Mug	$10.00
Shuttles from hotel to Disney World and Universal	Free
Entrance to Sea World	$85.00
Small bag of chips in Sea World	$3.00
Round trip shuttle from hotel to Sea World	$15.00

I Need My Space

I originally planned to spend five days in Orlando then return home, until a couple from Michigan informed me they were in town to watch the space shuttle launch. THERE WAS GOING TO BE A SPACE SHUTTLE LAUNCH? HOW FRICKIN COOL IS THAT?

It was Monday and the launch was scheduled for Thursday February 24th, 2011 at 4:50 pm so I promptly logged onto hotels.com and booked a room at a less expensive hotel for a week. I assumed the space center would be a zoo on launch day, if I could even get a ticket, so I decided to rent a car and drive to a nearby beach to watch the launch then visit the center a few days later once the crowds had dispersed.

After I settled into my new abode I went about the arduous task of renting a car. Unbeknownst to me, this was the final flight of the space shuttle Discovery and one of the few remaining launches of any space shuttle because the program was coming to an end.

People from all around the world had flooded into the area to witness this historical moment and rental cars were nearly impossible to find.

Space Shuttle Program

Officially called the Space Transportation System, NASA's Space Shuttle Program which was started in the late 1960's manages the only winged manned spacecraft to achieve orbit and landing. The reusable orbiter crafts are launched vertically carrying up to 8 astronauts and 50,000 pounds of payload into orbit with the help of two reusable solid rocket boosters (SBR) and an expendable external tank (ET) containing liquid hydrogen and liquid oxygen.

The SBR's are removed from the craft by explosive bolts about 2 minutes after liftoff and are parachuted into the ocean where they are recovered by ships and refurbished for reuse. The ET remains with the orbiter until it reaches 17,500 mph, the speed necessary for low Earth orbit.

▲ *The Discovery had a successful final launch and will be retiring after she returns to Earth.*

▲ *The final launch of the Discovery was a success.*

At this time the main engines are shut down and the ET is jettisoned downward where it burns upon re-entry into the Earth's atmosphere.

After completion of the mission (most of which last from several days to two weeks) it is then able to independently remove itself from orbit by means of its Maneuvering System and re-enter the Earth's atmosphere. During reentry, the orbiter heats up to over 1,500 degrees Celsius and would disintegrate were it not for the thermal protective system which includes LI-900 Silica ceramics that cover its underside.

Once in the lower atmosphere the orbiter acts like a conventional glider except that it has a much higher descent rate. Aerodynamic braking slows it down from 424 mph to 215 mph at touchdown compared to 160 mph for a jet airliner. The landing gear is lowered prior to touchdown and a drag chute is deployed to slow the craft down once on the runway.

The Vision for Space Exploration, announced by President George W. Bush in 2004, called for the space program to complete the International Space Station by 2010 and then retire the Space Shuttle to make way for the development of a new crew exploration vehicle that would enable manned missions to Mars and beyond.

Discovery's Final Flight

With the shuttle program coming to an end, the opportunities to watch a shuttle launch were becoming fewer and fewer. After the Discovery, the Endeavor has once more flight on the manifest and the Atlantis has the possibility of another flight and that may be the end. People had flooded into Orlando from all over the world to witness the launch.

The Daytona 500, a NASCAR race had just ended on the Sunday and many race fans also remained in town to watch the launch. Needless to say, finding a car to take me to one of the viewing sites 50 miles away proved to be a challenge to say the least.

I inquired at a number of places only to find out they had no cars available and every bus tour out to the space center had been sold out months in advance. It was the day before the launch and I still hadn't found a ride and was starting to lose hope of seeing my first and last space shuttle launch.

After getting a no from the rental company at my hotel, I was walking over to the nearby Starbucks to drown my sorrows in a latte when I heard a voice ask me if I needed any attraction tickets. I told the gentleman working the ticket booth about my shuttle dilemma then asked if by chance he had a tour going out to the launch site. He said no but suggested I ask the concierge at my hotel for help. I had assumed she would only direct me to the rental company in the booth beside her so I never bothered but perhaps there was a chance she could help.

I took a u-turn back to my hotel and much to my delight the concierge was able to arrange a car through a company called EZ-Rental - the name was fitting. First thing the following morning they picked me up from my hotel and drove me to their office which just happened to be on the way to the Kennedy Space Center. Within a few hours I was in Titusville waiting for the launch.

It was only noon giving me almost five hours to kill until launch time so, not wanting to burn in the searing heat, I did what women do best: shop.

I wanted something that would forever remind me of that special day and I found it at the JC Penny down the street from the empty lot where I was parked. It was a sterling silver ring that had the word Faith engraved into it and on the inside read, "Live by faith not by sight." How appropriate I thought but when I checked the price it was $50…a significant amount more than I was willing to pay for a souvenir. I was about to put it down when I noticed a sign saying 60% off. I brought it to the checkout counter and when the lady told me it was only $20, I knew that ring was meant for my finger.

I took it as the Universe reminding me to trust, something I had been working on since before my trip. I know you need to believe it to see it, not the other way around and thankfully the pioneers of space travel felt the same way or there would be no shuttle.

Thirty minutes before launch I scoured the beachfront in search of the perfect place to watch. Unlike the beautiful sandy Cocoa Beach where many like to witness launches, the waterfront in Titusville was filled with marshes and reeds but I was still able to secure a tiny patch of white sand to set up my towel and plunk my butt down. With only seconds to go, I focused my camera on what I thought was the launch pad and saw absolutely nothing. Thankfully I pulled my face up from the lens long enough to see everyone pointing to the left at a ball of fire pushing its way up from the ground. With no time to spare, I quickly focused on my new target and managed to get a few shots and some video before it got too far away. After all, it only takes the shuttle 8 minutes to reach space. The after two days in orbit they dock at the International Space Station.

About 5 minutes after the launch I raced to my car to get a jump on traffic. The news reports had estimate over 40,000 people expected to show up for the launch making traffic a nightmare. If I had any idea I would be stuck in traffic for 6 hours inching my way 50 miles back to Orlando I am not sure if I would have rented a car for $100, spent $26 on gas and hung out for five hours all for 4 minutes of excitement. Thank God I had no idea because I may have missed my chance to witness history in the making. This was the final flight of the Discovery and the second to last space shuttle mission.

Arriving at the Kennedy Space Center in 1983, Discovery was the third in a fleet of orbiters which included: Enterprise, Columbia, Challenger, Discovery, Atlantis and Endeavour.

Discovery's last mission, STS-133 was to attach the Permanent Multi-Purpose Module (PMM) to the International Space Station. It also carried the third of 4 ExPRESS Logistic Carriers (ELC) as well as Robonaut. What's all this high tech Star Trek stuff you ask? I admit I had to consult Wikipedia because I had absolutely no clue. Let me translate.

The PMM is primarily used for storage of spare supplies and waste. Basically it's a space garbage can and closet in one. The ELC is an un-pressurized attached payload platform that provides mechanical mounting surfaces, electrical power and command and data handling services for science experiments. In other words it is a science lab where science geeks can do science experiments.

Robonaut is a humanoid robot designed to work alongside the astronauts. He is like C-3PO from Star Wars.

So basically the mission was both historic and important and it was well worth the slowest drive in recorded history to witness. I could finally check watch a space shuttle launch off my bucket list.

▲ *The spacesuit that Gus Grissom wore on his Mercury flight is on display at the Astronaut Hall of Fame*

Discovery *Fast* Facts

- ✓ *Since its inaugural flight on August 30th 1984, Discovery has completed 39 successful missions surpassing all the other NASA orbiters in number of flights.*
- ✓ *Discovery carried the Hubble Space Telescope into space in 1990 and did two missions to service the telescope.*
- ✓ *Discovery was the first to fly after both the Challenger and Columbia disasters.*
- ✓ *The first member of royalty in space, Sultan bin Salman bin Abdulaziz Al Saud – the grandson of King Ibn Saud of Saudi Arabia, was carried aboard the Discovery.*
- ✓ *In 1998 Discovery carried 77-year old senator John Glenn into space making him the oldest person to fly in space.*
- ✓ *In 2010, the shuttle was the first to have three women on the crew who met up with a fourth at the space station setting another record of having four women in orbit.*
- ✓ *Discovery will be the first of the shuttle fleet to retire.*
- ✓ *Discovery had the honour of flying the 100th space shuttle mission STS-92*
- ✓ *Discovery will replace the space shuttle Enterprise in the Smithsonian's display at the Steven F. Udvar-Hazy Center.*

▲ *The US Astronaut Hall of Fame*

Astronauts Hall of Fame

A few days later, once everyone had gone home and the streets and amusement parks around Orlando went back to their normal levels of busy, I booked a shuttle (not a space shuttle just a normal one) to the Kennedy Space Center.

I started my visit at the United States Astronaut Hall of Fame – a museum honoring America's astronauts and housing the world's largest collection of their personal memorabilia. The idea of the Hall of Fame was conceived in the 1980's by the six then-surviving members of the Mercury Seven. Who was the Mercury Seven you ask? Good question. Also called the Original Seven and Astronaut Group 1, the Mercury Seven was the group of astronauts selected by NASA on April 9, 1959 to fly in the first manned spacecrafts as part of the Mercury Project. The group consisted of Alan Shepard (the first American in space), Virgil Grissom (the second American in space), John Herschel (the first American to orbit the Earth), Malcolm Carpenter (the second American to orbit the Earth), Walter Schirra, (the first person to go into space three times) Leroy Cooper (the first American to sleep in orbit and the last American to be launched alone into orbit) and Donald Kent.

The Mercury Seven were the first people to be inducted into the United States Astronaut Hall of Fame to be later joined by the thirteen astronauts from the Gemini and Apollo programs including Neil Armstrong (the first man to walk on the moon), Eugene Cernan (the last man to walk on the moon), Ed White (the first American to walk in space), Jim Lovell (commander of the famously near-tragic Apollo 13) and John Young (commander of the first Space Shuttle mission). In 2003, Sally Ride (the first American woman in space) was also inducted into the Hall of Fame.

One of the coolest exhibits was the Sigma 7, the spacecraft piloted by Walter Schirra when he made six orbits of the Earth on October 3rd 1962, in a 9-hour flight. The mission's goal was technical evaluation rather than scientific experimentation and it was considered a success.

Our driver had warned us not to ride in the G-Force Trainer if we had weak stomachs and were prone to motion sickness but when I saw the machine I forgot all about his warning. I needed to know if my body could handle space travel so I took a spin. The ride simulates the pressure of four times the force of gravity and a space shuttle landing. Two people ride in two separate capsules that spin on an arm rising up and down. I managed to complete the ride without hurling but I walked out of my capsule as though I was drunk – all the spinning had left me feeling dizzy.

I ended my visit at a display honouring the men and women who lost their lives in the name of space exploration including the crews from the Apollo 1, Challenger and Columbia.

▲ *Apollo 1 crew members from left to right: Virgil Grissom, Edward White, and Roger Chaffee*

Apollo One

On January 27th 1967, during a launch simulation test to prepare for their planned February 21st launch, a cabin fire broke out killing all three crew members. The Apollo One was to be the first manned mission of the lunar landing program with Virgil Grisson as the Command Pilot, Edward White as Senior Pilot and Roger Chaffee as Pilot. The test was riddled with delays such as issues with the communications between the pilots and the complex 34 blockhouse as well as high oxygen flow problems in the cabin. The cause of the fire remains unknown but at 6:30 pm the crew announced they were on fire. By the time the ground crew could contain it and reach the astronauts it was too late.

The investigation that followed revealed there was a lot of substandard wiring and plumbing in the craft which could have led to a fire however no ignition source was ever officially determined. They also discovered flammable materials in the cockpit including 34 square feet of Velcro which was found to be explosive in a high-pressure 100% oxygen environment. It was also found that the higher than ambient cabin pressure made it impossible for the crew to remove the inward-opening hatch to escape until the excess cabin pressure had been vented. Unfortunately that was not possible because Grissom, whose job it was to open the cabin vent was closest to the fire's point of origin and unable to do this.

As a result, the project was delayed for 20 months while the Command Module, which was found to be extremely hazardous and carelessly assembled, was redesigned and all manned missions went on to use the newly modified Block II spacecrafts. The cabin atmosphere at launch was changed from 100% oxygen to 60% oxygen and 40% nitrogen at sea-level pressure. Flammable materials in the cabin were replaced with self-extinguishing versions, plumbing and wiring were covered with protective insulation and the nylon used in the Block I space suits were replaced with a non-flammable, highly-resistant fabric woven from fiberglass and coated with Teflon.

▲ *The Challenger crew: (front row) Michael J. Smith, Dick Scobee, Ronald McNair; (back row) Ellison Onizuka, Christa McAuliffe, Gregory Jarvis, Judith Resnik*

Challenger Disaster

Seventy-three seconds into its flight on January 28th 1966, the Space Shuttle Challenger exploded killing all seven crew members and causing the space program to go on a 32-month hiatus while investigators tried to determine the cause of the tragedy.

The Rogers Commission, a special commission appointed by then president Ronald Reagan, investigated the accident and discovered that an O-ring seal failure on the right solid rocket booster allowed hot gas to reach the outside which affected the other rocket booster and lead to the structural failure of the external fuel tank. The exact timing of the crew's death is unknown however; several of the crew members survived the initial break-up of the craft but were unable to escape and may have been killed on impact when the crew compartment hit the ocean surface. The exact cause and timing of death of the astronauts has never been positively determined.

The commission also uncovered a flaw in NASA's organizational culture and decision making processes that led to the disaster. Managers had known about the potentially catastrophic flaw in the O-rings but failed to properly address it. They also disregarded engineer's warnings regarding the dangers of launching at such a cold temperature and, in an effort to maintain the launch schedule, failed to report the warnings to their superiors.

Adding to the tragedy of the whole event was the fact that school kids from all over the United States were watching the launch on television to cheer on Christa McAuliffe, the first member of the Teacher in Space Project – a NASA program announced by Ronald Reagan in 1984 designed to inspire students to pursue careers in mathematics, science and space exploration. Needless to say the program was cancelled after the incident. Unfortunately the changes that came about in regards to safety at NASA as a result were shallow and short-lived as was illustrated by the Space Shuttle Columbia disaster in 2003. The Columbia Accident Investigation Board concluded that NASA failed to learn the lessons taught by the Challenger disaster stating that the "same flawed decision making process" resulted in the Columbia disaster.

▲ *From left to right: David Brown, Rick Husband, Laurel Clark, Kalpana Chawla, Michael Anderson, William McCool, Ilan Ramon*

Columbia Disaster

On February 1st 2003, shortly before it was scheduled to conclude its 28th mission, the Space Shuttle Columbia disintegrated in the skies above Texas during re-entry into the Earth's atmosphere resulting in the deaths of all seven crew members. At first, some suspected terrorism due to the fact that the shuttle was carrying the first ever Israeli astronaut, but there was no evidence to support that theory. However, evidence did support the theory that the tragedy was a result of damage sustained during launch when a small piece of foam insulation broke off the external tank and struck the edge of the left wing causing damage to the craft's thermal protection system. The problem was detected while they were in orbit but NASA management refused to further investigate on the grounds that little could be done even if the damage was found. While the original shuttle design specifications clearly stated that debris was not to shed from the external tank and that these issues needed to be resolved before a launch was cleared, launches were given the go ahead regardless because engineers came to see the foam shedding and debris strikes as inevitable and not a threat to safety. Apparently they were wrong because during re-entry, the damaged area allowed hot gases to penetrate and destroy the internal wing structure causing rapid in-flight break-up of the craft.

The remains of the shuttle and crew scattered over parts of Texas, Louisiana and Arkansas. Space shuttle flights and the construction of the International Space Station were put on hold for two years as the Columbia Accident Investigation Board determined the cause of the disaster.

It was concluded that there was a possibility for a rescue mission since Columbia was carrying an unusually large quantity of consumables as part of its Extended Duration Orbiter package which would have allowed the astronauts to survive for thirty days. Normally it would take much longer than this to prepare another shuttle for launch but because the Atlantis was well along processing due to its impending launch this was not a problem. The crew could have been saved but not the shuttle since, at that time, they could not land by remote control. It would have crashed into the ocean. The investigation commission recommended a number of safety measures to incorporate into future space craft designs including an automatic parachute system that would allow astronauts a better chance to escape and survive a damaged shuttle. Countless memorials and tributes to the astronauts were made including seven newly discovered asteroids named after the crew members as well as a number of buildings and roads renamed to honour them.

Astronaut Encounter

We arrived at the Kennedy Space Center, which is a short drive from the Hall of Fame, at 10:45 am giving me just enough time to make my way over to Astronaut Encounter and secure a front row seat for a presentation given by an astronaut.

Expecting an elderly gentleman with gray hair wearing a flight suit and reading glasses, I was surprised when an attractive blonde woman in her early 50's walked onto the stage.

I can't believe I am still stuck in that age-old belief around careers for men and women. If I had been told a nurse or secretary was giving a lecture I would have expected a woman but space travel seemed like a man's career hence that's what I had expected.

When Susan Kilrain started talking I loved her right away. She wasn't much different than me thus confirming my belief that I could visit space one day as well. If John Glenn could meet NASA's physical and mental requirements for space travel at age 77, I still had plenty of time.

Kilrain had a military naval aviator background working as a flight instructor and later as a test pilot logging over 3,000 flight hours in over 30 different aircraft. She reported to the Johnson Space Center as an Astronaut Candidate in 1995 where she piloted two space shuttle missions logging over 900 hours in space.

In her 30-minute video-slide show presentation, Susan told us what it was like to be part of a shuttle mission. For seven days prior to launch she and the crew were quarantined and not even allowed to see their families in order to ensure no one got sick prior to the mission. A few days before launch the crew flew from the Johnson Space Center in Houston where they are trained to the Kennedy Space Center in T-38 Talon trainers. These twin engine, high-altitude supersonic jets are used by NASA to train pilot astronauts.

On launch day they are brought over to the launch pad in the astrovan where they ride an elevator up to the cockpit of the orbiter.

Six seconds before launch the engines start and when the computers determine the engines are working properly they command the solid rocket boosters to fire. Once they are lit there is no turning back, you are on your way to space.

They are traveling at 100 miles per hour before they even leave the launch pad although to observers it appears as though they are standing still. After only 30 seconds they are traveling faster than the speed of sound.

▲ *Susan Kilrain has piloted 2 space shuttle missions.*

The ride is bumpy and Susan said they felt like a bunch of rocks jumping around inside the space shuttle. The rockets stay attached for two minutes at which point they run out of fuel and jettison off the shuttle parachuting into the Atlantic Ocean where they are retrieved by boat. After eight and a half minutes they are in orbit around 200-300 miles above the Earth's surface.

During one of the missions she and the crew did science experiments for 16 days, 24-hours a day. Some of the experiments included mixing different metals together to create new alloys hoping to find metals that are less corrosive and stronger for us to use on Earth.

Susan went on to describe daily life in the space station and how they ate, slept and exercised. They had a sleep station that resembled shelves in a morgue where the astronauts would slide into sleeping bags and strap themselves down to best simulate a bed. Unfortunately the body is not used to sleeping in a weightless state making it difficult to sleep in space. Because your muscles don't have to work against gravity, they go on vacation when you are in space and therefore exercise is important. They have bicycle trainers to work out on as well as resistance training equipment that they are required to use every day. Most of the food is dehydrated which they rehydrate. Since there is no gravity it is fun to play with food in space. A juice bubble splattered against a wall can turn into hundreds of tiny juice balls.

When the mission was over and it was time to return to the Earth, first they had to reenter the Earth's Atmosphere at which time the craft heated up to 2000-3000 degrees Celsius but thanks to the black tiles on the underside of the craft they did not disintegrate. Although the shuttle resembles a plane, it has no engines and is actually a 200,000 pound glider which is like a brick falling from the sky.

They have to keep their speed and altitude up high to conserve enough energy to make it to the runway giving them one chance to get it right. That is why they make their descent at 20 degrees as opposed to the 1 or 2 degree descent of a jetliner. Once they get to 2000 feet over the ground they slowly start to raise the nose up. Until that time it looks like they are going to crash. Thankfully she and the crew managed to land the shuttle safely and head out to the runway to do their press conference before heading back to their accommodations for a much needed shower.

After the presentation Susan posed for pictures with people and I of course was first in line. Yes I felt a bit guilty racing in front of the swarm of kids to get there first but I was bigger and faster and won fair and square.

▲ *The Discovery was launched from pad 39A.*

▲ *The large building on the left is the Vehicle Assembly Building where the shuttle is assembled before being brought to the launch pad via the Crawlerway, the road in front of it that leads to the launch pad.*

Launch Complex 39

After getting my picture taken with an astronaut, I hopped on a bus that took me to the viewing platform at Launch Complex 39.

Composed of two launch pads, the Vehicle Assembly Building and the Crawlerway, the Orbiter Processing Facility, the Launch Control Center, a News Facility and other support buildings, this is where the space shuttle is assembled and launched.

After the orbiter returns from a mission it is towed from the Shuttle Landing Facility to one of three Orbiter Processing Centers at Launch Complex 39 to undergo maintenance. It takes several months to remove any remaining payloads from the craft, inspect, test and refurbish it. If it is being prepared for another mission then a few weeks before launch mission flight kits are installed and consumable fluids and gases are added where possible. Any remaining payloads, fuels and fluids are installed on the pad closer to launch day.

The orbiter is then brought to the Vehicle Assembly Building (VAB) to be mated with the solid rocket boosters and the external fuel tanks and flight hardware to become a space shuttle.

The VAB is 526 feet tall and 518 ft wide making it the largest single story building in the world with an interior so huge it has its own weather including rain clouds that form below the ceiling on very humid days. It is equipped with five overhead bridge cranes two of which are capable of lifting 250 tons.

Once assembled, the shuttle is transported to the launch site via the Crawlerway – a 100 foot wide double pathway. The crawler-transporter, a large pair of tracked vehicles is used to transport the shuttle. Traveling at a maximum speed of one mile per hour, it takes about five to eight hours to transport the shuttle down the 3.5 mile long Crawlerway. The same two crawlers nicknamed Hanz and Franz (after two bodybuilding characters from Saturday Night Live) have been used since they were delivered in 1965. The 2,721 ton vehicles which measure 131 ft by 114 ft and adjust from 20ft to 26ft high, each have 8 tracks with 57 shoes that weigh almost 2000 pounds each.

With the help of its laser guidance system and a levelling system, it is able to keep the two Mobile Launcher Platforms (on which the shuttle sits) level within 10 minutes

of arc while moving it to the launch site – quite a feat considering each is two stories high and weighs 8,230,000 pounds.

Once at the pad, the MLP is lowered onto several pedestals and the Crawler-Transporter doubles its speed to 2 miles per hour and makes its way to a staging area.

There are two launch pads however LC-39B was deactivated in 2007 while the future of LC-39A remains uncertain after the shuttle program ends in 2011. Each pad contains a Fixed Service Structure (FSS) and a Rotating Service Structure (RSS). The FSS gives access to the shuttle through retractable arms while the RSS contains the Payload Changeout Room which offers access to the orbiter's payload bay and protects the shuttle from winds of up to 110 km/h.

Swing arms give access to different parts of the shuttle. They include the Orbiter Access Arm to access the crew module, the Gaseous Oxygen Vent Arm that positions a hood over the top of the External tank for fueling and a Hydrogen Vent Line Access Arm that mates the External Tank Ground Umbilical Carrier Plate to the launch pad hydrogen vent line.

Also located at the pads are large cryogenic tanks where the liquid hydrogen and liquid oxygen fuel is stored. These fuels are highly explosive and that is why the safe distance for a fully fueled Space Shuttle is three mile. Before tanking operations begin, all non-essential workers are evacuated from the danger area as a precaution.

Each pad is serviced by an elevated 300,000 gallon water tank to provide sound buffering protection for the launch. During lift-off the water is released as a safely measure to muffle the intense sound waves. It produces the large amount of steam visible during launch.

The bus dropped us off in front of a three story viewing platform with an excellent view of the complex. I have seen documentaries on space shuttle launches but seeing the facility first hand really put things into perspective. I could totally see myself pulling up to the launch pad in an atrovan, getting into a shuttle and going to space.

As I looked over at the launch pad, I regretted not visiting the center before the launch when I could have seen the space shuttle sitting on the pad. However, when I looked around at the crowds and imagined how large they were days before I quickly got over my regrets.

There was a lot to see and I only had 6 hours to see it. Had I visited before the launch I would have spent most of my time in lineups and may have missed many of the sights.

When I was done, I got into the non-existent line for the bus and headed over to the Apollo/Saturn V Center.

▲ *The American flag on the side of the Vehicle Assembly Building is 209 feet high and 110 feet wide. The blue area alone is the size of a regulation basketball court.*

▲ *Buzz Aldrin, pilot of the Lunar Module, was the second man to walk on the moon.*

Apollo/Saturn V Center

My visit to the Apollo/Saturn Center started with 2 short films, one simulating the environment inside the Apollo firing room during an Apollo launch and the other simulating the first moon landing. I went into the complex where I was blown away by the huge Saturn V rocket hanging from the ceiling. Because it was an expendable rocket meaning that after it left the command module it disintegrated on its way back to Earth, the Saturn on display had never been to space rather it was the rocket that would have been used for the cancelled Apollo 19 mission. Amongst the other treasures on display were the original Mercury Control consoles that were removed before the original building was demolished, as well as an unused Lunar Module, Alan Shepard's Corvette and Apollo 14 spacesuit and a moon rock that visitors can touch. I was excited to see these artifacts from one of the most memorable times in world history. I am sure anyone alive at that time remembers where they were when Neil Armstrong uttered those famous words, "That's one small step for man, one giant leap for mankind."

Hours after the United States launched their first man into space in 1961 President John F. Kennedy announced a national goal of landing a man on the moon. The Soviets were winning the space race, one of many silent battles during the Cold War, with two major victories: Sputnik 1 – the first satellite into space and Yuri Gararin – the first human to travel into space. The Americans were scrambling to catch up and gain supremacy in outer space and if the Apollo Program was successful, it would push them into the lead. This goal was accomplished by the Apollo 11 mission on July 20, 1969 when Neil Armstrong and Buzz Aldrin landed on the moon while Michael Collins remained in lunar orbit.

Before entering the space program, Neil Armstrong (born August 5, 1930) had served in the US Navy seeing action in the Korean War.

▲ *The Apollo 14 command module is on display at the Apollo/Saturn V Center.*

After the war he served as a test pilot flying over 900 flights in a variety of aircraft and, in 1957, he was selected by the US Air Force to join their space program.

When Armstrong heard NASA was accepting applications for a second group of astronauts he applied. However, his application arrived a week after the deadline. Thankfully his buddy Dick Day noticed the late application and slipped it into the pile unnoticed. On September 13th 1962, Deke Slayton invited Armstrong to be part of the New Nine and without hesitation Armstrong accepted.

Armstrong's first mission was aboard the Gemini 8 as its Command Pilot. Project Gemini's objectives were to develop techniques for advanced space travel in preparation for the Apollo Program. Their missions included the first American spacewalk as well as new orbital maneuvers including rendezvous and docking with another spacecraft. It was this program that tested the ability of humans and equipment to endure extended periods of spaceflight and provided astronauts with the zero gravity, rendezvous and docking experience they would need to make Apollo a success. In total there were 12 Gemini flights including two unmanned flights which were all launched by Titan II rockets.

Armstrong was in Washington, D.C. on January 27th 1967 when fire broke out in the Apollo 1 killing the three-man crew. On April 5th 1967 he was assigned to the backup crew for Apollo 9 but after design and manufacturing delays Apollo 9 and Apollo 8 swapped crews putting Armstrong in line to command Apollo 11 based on the normal crew rotation.

On December 23rd 1968 while the Apollo 8 (which Armstrong was named commander of the backup crew) orbited the Earth, Slayton offered Armstrong the position of commander of Apollo 11, the first mission to land on the moon. Much to the dismay of Aldrin who thought he would be the first man to walk on the moon, Armstrong was given the honor for two reasons. The official reason given was because the design of the Lunar Module made it more practical for Armstrong to exit the capsule ahead of Aldrin. Unofficially, it was thought that Armstrong's lack of a large ego made him a better candidate.

Due to a problem with the computers, Armstrong had to manually control the Lumar Module in order to make a safe landing since they had overshot the original landing site. He managed to land with only 30 seconds of fuel left. The capsule touched down on the moon at 20:17:39 UTC on July 20th 1969 and Armstrong radioed to Mission Control, "Houston, Tranquility Base here. The Eagle has landed."

While Armstrong may have been the first man to step on the moon, Aldrin ended up in most of the photographs since Armstrong was also the cameraman. There are only five images of Armstrong and none of them are anything to write home about. All of the iconic images of a man walking on the moon were ones taken by Armstrong of Aldrin. Aldrin was going to take a picture of Armstrong but was interrupted by a communication by President Nixon.

The pair were only allotted 2.5 hours outside the module during which time they planted an American flag, set up the Early Apollo Scientific Experimentation Package and left a small package of memorial items in honor of deceased Soviet cosmonauts Yuri Gagarin (the first man in space) who died in a plane crash and Vladimir

Komarov, the first human to die during a space mission as well as the Apollo 1 astronauts. Subsequent missions were allotted up to and over 21 hours of moon exploration.

In preparing to leave the moon, the pair discovered they had broken the ignition switch for the ascent engine but in a move of pure MacGyver, they managed to use part of a pen to push the circuit breaker and activate the launch sequence. Aldrin kept the pen and has it displayed in a glass case. The Lunar Module then docked with the Columbia, its command and service module and returned to the Earth splashing down in the Pacific Ocean.

After spending 18 days in quarantine to make sure they didn't bring back any moon diseases, the crew traveled across the United States as part of the 45-day Giant Leap tour.

How does one top walking on the moon? Having achieved such career success so early in life it is hard to imagine what a guy could possibly do next. Armstrong however managed to maintain a successful career serving on the board of directors in such companies as United Airlines and Eaton Corporation and acting as a spokesman for Chrysler and Marathon Oil. He also spent 8 years teaching in the University of Cincinnati's Department of Aerospace Engineering.

Rocket Garden

I arrived back at the Visitor's Center just in time for a guided tour of the Rocket Garden which featured mock-up capsules from the Mercury, Gemini and Apollo programs as well as eight milestone launch vehicles from both manned and unmanned missions including the Mercury-Redstone, Mercury-Atlas and the Titan II.

▲ *A Saturn V rocket hangs from the ceiling of the Apollo/Saturn V Center.*

Mercury-Redstone – The Mercury-Redstone was the rocket that launched Ham the Astrochimp and Alan Shepard into space. On May 5th 1961, Shepard became the first American launched into space after piloting the Freedom 7 mission, a 16 minute flight that attained an altitude of just over 187 kilometers. He landed in the Atlantic Mission Range where he was collected by a helicopter and celebrated as a national hero and honored with parades in Washington, New York and Los Angeles. Prior to launch he said to himself: "Don't fuck up, Shepard". The quote evolved into what is now known amongst aviators as Shepard's Prayer: "Dear Lord, please don't let me fuck up."

Shepard went on to be the fifth man to walk on the moon, serve on the board of directors of many corporations and became a millionaire. In 1994, he published a book called

Moon Shot: The Inside Story of America's Race to the Moon before dying of leukemia in 1998.

The Freedom 7 command module was placed on display in the lobby of the Armel-Leftwich Visitor Center at the U.S. Naval Academy in Annapolis, MD after Shepard's death. Ham the Chimp lived out the rest of his days in the National Zoo in Washington, D.C. and the North Carolina Zoo before his death at age 26 in 1983.

Mercury-Atlas – The Mercury-Atlas rockets were Intercontinental Ballistic Missiles redesigned to work as launch rockets and credited for launching the first American into orbit. On February 20th 1962, astronaut John Glenn piloted the Friendship 7 on a four hour and 56 minute flight that orbited the Earth 3 times before re-entering the Earth's atmosphere and splashing down into the Atlantic Ocean.

In July of the same year, Glenn testified before the House Space Committee in favor of excluding women from the NASA astronaut program. It wasn't until 1983 that NASA flew the first American female astronaut Sally Ride into space and it was not until 1993 when Eileen Collins became the first woman to pilot a NASA mission.

The Soviet space program was much friendlier to woman having the honor of sending the first woman into space. On June 16th 1963, cosmonaut Valentina Tereshkova piloted the Vostok 6 on a three-day mission to collect data on the female body's reaction to spaceflight.

Not only was she the first woman in space she was also the first civilian in space. Before being recruited as a cosmonaut, Valentina worked in a textile factory and was an amateur parachutist.

▲ *The Rocket Garden features eight milestone launch vehicles from the American space program.*

Titan II – The Titan II was an expendable launch system derived from the Titan II missile used to launch 12 Gemini missions, two unmanned and twelve manned. Its claim to fame was the Gemini IV mission which included the first American space walk. On June 7th 1965, astronaut Edward White floated free tethered to the outside of the spacecraft for twenty minutes. Unfortunately he missed the opportunity to be the first human to walk in space as that honor went to his Soviet counterpart cosmonaut Aleksei Leonov a few months earlier.

While he was outside the craft, his spare thermal glove floated away making him one of, if not the first human to litter in space. Thankfully it burned up upon its reentry into the Earth's atmosphere leaving no evidence of the crime. White also came close to becoming a piece of space debris after encountering a mechanical problem with the hatch mechanism in the capsule. Since they could not re-enter the Earth's atmosphere with an unsealed hatch they may have literally been lost in space. Thankfully they were able to pull a MacGyver and White and James McDivitt made a safe return. White's luck ran out in 1967 when he died in a cabin fire during a pre-launch test along with the other two astronauts on the crew of the Apollo 1.

Shuttle Launch Experience

Unfortunately I was running out of time and did not get the chance to see the two IMAX films Hubble 3D (about the Hubble Space Telescope) and Space Station 3D (about the International Space Station). Instead I went on the Shuttle Launch Experience – a virtual ride that simulates launching into orbit on a space shuttle.

I, along with several other "touristonauts" entered the Shuttle Launch Simulation Facility, a six-story structure resembling the actual Space Shuttle facility in the Kennedy Space Center.

The $60 million attraction was built with the help of astronauts, NASA experts and attraction-industry leaders. The building houses four simulators that each accommodates 44 people. This is about as close as it gets to a launch simulation.

During the pre-launch briefing Space Shuttle Commander Charlie Bolden took us step-by-step through the shuttle launch sequence. We were then brought into the shuttle where we experienced the rockets firing and lift off.

We shook about in our seats feeling the rumble of the powerful rockets until we reached orbit where everything went silent and we had the sensation of zero gravity as our bodies pushed forward to escape from our seats.

As the Earth came into view amongst a sky full of stars, Elton John's song Rocket Man came to mind.

She packed my bags last night pre-flight
Zero hour nine a.m.
And I'm gonna be high as a kite by then
I miss the earth so much I miss my wife
It's lonely out in space
On such a timeless flight
And I think it's gonna be a long long time
Till touchdown brings me round again to find
I'm not the man they think I am at home
Oh no no no I'm a rocket man
Rocket man burning out his fuse up

I ended the day with a visit to the souvenir shop where I bought a shooter glass that read, "I Need My Space" to go along with the one I had bought at the Johnson Space Center that read, "It's Not Rocket Science" (oh wait, yes it is). When I got back to the bus all I could think of was how I wanted to return one day so I could see the IMAX movies, train like an astronaut and have lunch with an astronaut. There was so much to do and not enough time for me to be a rocket woman.

▲ *A life sized mock orbiter is on display at the Space Center that visitors can walk inside.*

Top Ten Crazy Space Facts

1. The Vehicle Assembly Building is the largest single story building in the world.
2. Astronauts wear diapers during the launch because they have to sit in the orbiter for hours before the launch without access to a bathroom and because of the pressure lift off acceleration puts on their bladder.
3. In 2005, Neil Armstrong's barber of 20 years sold some of his hair to a collector for $3000. Armstrong threatened legal action if the barber did not return the hair or donate the money to the astronaut's charity of choice. The barber chose option B.
4. Valeri Polyakov currently holds the record for the longest single human spaceflight having spent 437 days 18 hours aboard the Soviet space station Mir in 1988.
5. In 1957 the Soviets launched the first animal into orbit, a dog named Laika. Unfortunately the technology to return to Earth had not yet been developed and she died in space from overheating in the fourth circuit of flight making her also the first animal to die in space. Her craft, Sputnik 2 disintegrated along with her remains over five months later while re-entering the Earth's atmosphere. The experiment paved the way for human spaceflight by proving that a living being could survive being launched into space and endure weightlessness.
6. In 1998, a space tourism company was established to offer zero-gravity atmospheric flights and orbital spaceflights with an option to participate in a spacewalk. So far 7 clients have been launched into space on missions to the International Space Station aboard Soviet spacecrafts.
7. American businessman Dennis Tito paid a reported $20 million to become the first space tourist.
8. In 2009, Cirque du Soleil founder Guy Laliberte became the first Canadian space tourist.
9. British business tycoon Richard Branson opened a company called Virgin Galactic that aims to provide space flights to civilians for $200,000 per passenger for a 2-hour sub-orbital flight.
10. The first attempt to reach Mars was in 1960 and in 1964, the US made the first successful flyby of the red planet and have since landed rovers and hope to one day land a man on Mars.

▲ *One of the films at the Apollo/Saturn V Center simulates the launch of Apollo 8, the first mission to reach the moon, on screens overtop of the actual control room consoles used during the Apollo Program.*

What Did Things Cost?

Items Purchased	American Dollars
One day car rental	$111.00
Toll Booth #1	$40.00
Toll Booth #2	$0.75
Toll Booth #3	$1.00
Gas	$20.00
Buffet Dinner at Golden Coral	$11.50
Kennedy Space Center Tour	$100.00
Souvenir NASA shooter glass	$4.00
Souvenir Space Center Coffee Mug	$8.00
Discovery Official Launch Program	$10.00
Commemorative Discovery Launch Coin	$5.00
Watching a Space Shuttle Launch	Priceless
Shuttle from hotel to airport	$21.00

There's No Place Like Home

Somewhere along the way I had found my happy and part of me feared losing it when I went back home. Was I able to go back to my life and still feel confident and good about myself? Not that I had a choice. My money had run out and the party was ending whether I was ready or not. On March 1st as I boarded the plane heading for Kamloops my mind drifted back to that night in Buenos Aires and the three wishes the people at my table had made for me. They wished for me to let go of my need to find love and learn to love myself, find a place to stay put for awhile and heal and see myself as the loving, adventurous and beautiful woman I am.

My eyes welled up with tears as I realized that their wishes had all come true. I did love myself and no longer required a relationship to validate me.

I stayed put in Orlando long enough to heal...or better yet realise that there was nothing wrong with me in the first place.

I felt like I had just awakened from a long sleep and was ready to face the world. I was me again and confident that I could handle whatever life threw at me. Bring it!

My parents picked me up at the airport and brought me home for some much needed rest. It felt good to be back in my house and even better to be reunited with my rabbit Jack. The weather was still cold and miserable but I wasn't.

In the past year I had learned how to meditate and I hoped that regular practice would help me to remain calm and confident. My mind wreaked havoc in my life and I was determined to gain some control over it so I could live in peace.

▲ *The name Kamloops means meeting of the rivers as it is located where the North Thompson meets the South Thompson.*

▲ *Here's a picture of me on the air guitar and Jason McCoy on a real guitar.*

Knowing that my ability to solve life's big problems was limited, I got into the habit of asking the Universe to help me. But if I wanted the Universe to give me advice, I needed t to not only ask but shut up and listen to it. That is where learning to stop the chatter in my head came in handy. Simple solutions to my most difficult problems were finally able to come through and life got a lot easier.

Jason McCoy Tickets

On New Year's Day I declared my word of the year was trust and after only three months I felt I was well on my way to trusting not only the Universe but myself and others as well. With nine months remaining in the year, I decided to add another word to my plate: fun.

The Universe fully supported my new word by bringing Canadian country singer Jason McCoy to town. Born on August 27th in Barrie, Ontario and raised in Camrose, Alberta, this singer/songwriter has won numerous awards including Canadian Country Music's 2001 Male Vocalist of the Year, 3 SOCAN song of the year awards, 19 CCMA nominations, 5 Juno nominations for Best Country Male Vocalist, 6 awards at the 2004 Ontario Country Performer and Fan Association awards and the Global Artist Award at the Country Music Awards in Nashville. Add to that countless chart toppers such as "This Used to Be Our Town", "Learning a Lot About Love" and "Born Again in Dixieland" and you have one Canadian Superstar.

In 2005, McCoy joined forces with Clayton Bellamy and Chris Bryne to form the band Road Hammers. The first sign of the band appeared in Paul Brant's video for the remake of Convoy. McCoy appears in the video wearing a Road Hammer's shirt. The band, whose first album The Road Hammers debuted at #1 on the Canadian country albums chart, also starred in a reality show of the same name on Canada's Country Music Television. After being nominated for six CCMA awards and winning Group or Duo of the year, the group disbanded after a final show in Langley, British Columbia on December 31st 2010.

I had run out of money and had to borrow some from my parents to pay my mortgage, so needless to say I wasn't able to pay the $40 cover charge. But the Universe had my back. On the morning of the concert a message came up on my Facebook homepage saying click like here to win two tickets to Jason McCoy. I did just that and two hours later I received an email stating that I had just won the tickets. How easy was that?

JASON MCCOY *FAST* FACT

Jason McCoy and Clayton Bellamy were contestants on the reality show Mantracker on September 6th 2010. The show features Terry Grant, an expert tracker, who pursues two individuals through the wilderness in Canada and the United States. The contestants, called prey, must elude capture and reach the finish line within 31 hours. Grant does not get to meet the contestants or know their destination. Jason and Clayton were able to make it to the finish line without getting caught.

I called up my buddy Monique and invited her to join me for a fun-filled evening of good old Canadian country music. I hadn't been to a concert in a long time because I don't like having to sit for three hours in a coliseum full of people but this concert wasn't like that. The venue was small and intimate so Jason was able to interact with the audience. He shared stories about his life and some of his ups and downs on his road to success and even shared old video footage of his 1980's mullet days. He could have given Billy Ray Cyrus, the Mullet King, a run for his money.

There was a dance floor in front of the stage and when he played "Born Again in Dixieland" me and my friends (I ran into a bunch of girls I know at the concert) got up to dance. Every since I got my "dance back" in Machu Picchu I wanted to dance with everyone everywhere.

Watching Jason rock the crowd brought back fond memories of my own days dabbling in the country music scene. In fact, I remembered him winning CCMA's Male Vocalist of the Year because I was in the audience. Yes you read that right…I was in the audience.

When I was 18 I learned how to play the guitar and shortly after that I turned my passion for writing poetry into a passion for writing songs. By my late 20's I had written dozen's of songs and wanted to take my passion to the next level so I decided to make my first demo.

I was living in Calgary at the time where I hired Rob at Rocky Mountain Studio to help me produce my first professional CD. He hired some musicians and I hired Calgary country singer Sandy D'acy to do vocals and within a week I had a three-song CD.

Beaming with pride, I wanted to market my songs to a publisher with hopes of becoming a professional song writer. When I heard about the Canadian Country Music Week taking place in Calgary, I figured that would be a great place to network and perhaps turn my dream a reality.

I went down to the hotel and convention center where the event was taking place to see if I could pick up tickets for any of the events and much to my delight, there was a president's ball taking place that night with one available ticket left.

▲ *Rob from Rocky Mountain Studio helped me record my first demo.*

▲ *Cam from BMG Records, me and Russell De Carle, the lead singer of Prairie Oyster hit the town.*

I figured that ticket must have been intended for me so I purchased it along with a ticket to the Canadian Country Music Awards and after party.

Needless to say I was a bit nervous about showing up to a black tie event solo. I had gone to movies alone and the occasional pub but this pushed even my comfort level. The tables were not assigned and I did not know anyone or so I thought.

Wearing a long sexy black dress, I entered the cocktail area and immediately spotted Sandy, the girl who sang on my demo and much to my surprise she was there with my roommate's ex-boyfriend. How weird is that? They invited me to sit with them and we shared a table with two Dee-jays from the country station's morning show.

The Dee-jays kept me well entertained throughout the dinner but the event ended early in the evening leaving me all dressed up with nowhere to go. Not ready to go home, I heard some music coming from a pub inside the hotel so I went to check it out. After standing in a line at the bar for 15 minutes, I reached the front only to find out that I had to purchase my drink tickets at a different location. The kind man behind me took pity and offered to buy me a drink while I stood and waited with his friend.

His friend was a tall lanky blonde man in his 50's who looked like he just stepped off the stage of the Grand Old Operay. He introduced himself as Russell deCarle and trying to make small talk I asked him if he was from town. When he said no he was from back East, I asked him what brought him to town. He said he came for country music week, so I went on to ask him what he did and he said he was with the band Prairie Oyster.

I loved their music and often heard it on the radio however I never watched country music television so I had no idea what my favourite artists looked like. I am sure the man thought I was a complete idiot when I asked him what instrument he played. In fact, I am pretty his buddy snickered as he handed me my drink and Russell announced he was the lead singer.

▲ *Julian Austin flexed his muscles for me.*

With a beet red face I apologized only to hear his buddy, who I later discovered was Cam, artist relations for BMG Records, tell me that was the best laugh he had all night.

For those of you who are unfamiliar with Prairie Oyster, they are a country band from Ontario who has been named Country Group or Duo of the year six times by both the CCMA and the Juno Awards. They have had four number one singles in Canada with an additional 12 singles reaching the Canadian Country Top 10 and eight albums certified gold or platinum by the Canadian Recording Industry Association.

When we finished our drinks, the pair invited me to hit the town and escorted me into a limousine that brought us to a small pub with live music. Russell introduced me to his friend Keith Glass and when I asked what he did he said he played the guitar. Not able to quit asking dumb questions, I asked him if he was any good, to which he replied, "Ask Russell, I am his lead guitar player". Yikes, two blunders in a roll, these people must have been wondering what the hell I was doing at Canadian Country Music's largest annual networking event with no clue as to who anyone was.

I'd like to say it ended there but that wasn't the case. I managed to go from dumb to dumber the following night when Cam and Russell invited me to the exclusive BMG records VIP party held in the Penthouse of the hotel. I showed up with my roommate Cari who was about as familiar with the faces of Canadian country music as I was.

When I ran into Cam, he made a point of introducing me to every famous person in the room wondering if I would recognize any of them. Apparently he found my ignorance a source of personal amusement. First he called over a handsome cowboy and whispered in my ear, "Ask him to take off his jacket". I put in the request and Julian Austin removed his jacket to reveal the sexiest set of pipes on the planet. After posing for a few arm-flexing pictures with me, his girlfriend cleared her throat to signify it was time for him to put his jacket back on and quit flirting with the blonde.

After Julian slunk off, a handsome man with long dirty blonde hair sat down to join us. Of course I did not recognize him as the former guitar/keyboard player for Men Without Hats but that didn't stop Stefan Doroschuk from singing me a few verses of Safety Dance – one of my all time favourite 80's songs.

He had taken a sabbatical from music and was working for BMG at the time but in his heyday, he and his brother lead singer Ivan Doroschuk started the 80's new wave band from Montreal.

Their hit Safety Dance spent four weeks at number three on the Billboard Hot 100 and also peaked at #6 on the UK singles chart and rated eleventh best selling single of the year in South Africa. However, in Canada it only reached #12 on the singles chart. What the…?

▲ *Stefan Doroschuk from Men Without Hats poses for a picture with my roommate Cari and Cam.*

In 1987, their single Pop Goes the World hit #20 on the Billboard Hot 100, #2 in the Canadian Chart and #1 in Australia.

Amongst the other celebrities in the room were Paul Brant and Beverley Mahood but I didn't recognize them either. That is until the following evening at the Canadian Country Music Awards where I recognized a number of people from the party as they went on stage to either present awards or accept them.

Hosted by Terri Clark, some of the top awards included:

Female Artist of the Year – Carolyn Dawn Johnson
Male Artist of the Year – Jason McCoy
Group or Dou of the Year – The Wilkinson's
Video of the Year – No Fear by Terri Clark
Music Hall of Fame Inductees – Gordon Lightfoot and Gary Buck
Guitar player of the year – Keith Glass of Prairie Oyster

I remembered watching Jason McCoy receive the award for Male Artist of the Year and I have been a huge fan ever since. Needless to say I had a fantastic time dancing with my friends at his concert. My first week home was going awesome. Life was good!

My Crazy Grandma

On Friday March 11, 2011 a 9.0 magnitude undersea megathrust earthquake called Tohoku hit off the coast of Japan. Having survived numerous earthquakes over the years, the country was well prepared and sustained relatively little damage However, little could have prepared them for the massive tsunami that was triggered. Waves reaching to heights of 37.9 meters travelled up to 10 kilometres inland wrecking havoc on everything in their way. There were over 12,000 confirmed deaths and over 15,000 people missing as well as 125,000 buildings damaged or destroyed. Millions of households were left without electricity, water, roads and train tracks were damaged and most disturbing of all was the damage caused at the Fukushima II Nuclear Power Plant.

A state of emergency was declared after the cooling systems at the plant failed. On March 12th an explosion caused by the build-up of hydrogen gas blew away the roof and outer walls of Reactor 1 and by the following day it was announced that a partial nuclear meltdown could be occurring in Reactor's 1 and 3.

The world watched in horror as workers scrambled to cool down the reactors and prevent a nuclear disaster. Everyone was worried about what could possibly happen if they didn't succeed…everyone but me that is. I don't worry about the big things. I figured if the world was going to end there was nothing I could do to stop it so oh well. I prefer to worry about stupid stuff like will I make it to my appointment on time, will he call me and will I lose that last ten pounds. How absurd is that?

My grandmother however is exactly the opposite; she doesn't worry about the day to day stuff because she is too busy worrying about whether or not the world is going to end. She had recently moved out of my parents' house and into a care home where she spent her days glued to CNN watching the drama in Japan unfold and preparing for the inevitable nuclear disaster that would end life as we know it. At least it took her mind off of her other favourite obsession: planning her own funeral. But it was annoying just the same.

My attempt to visit her and tell her about my big trip was interrupted with her pleas for me to fill up all my plastic jugs with tap water because radiation from Japan could seep into the river and ruin our drinking water. Yes, my grandma is crazy. She honestly believed that a few jugs of water would save her in the event of a nuclear disaster. How does one argue with crazy? Are all grandmas' nuts or just mine?

I wanted to throw her television out the window because the world news seemed to be going from bad to worse. Added to the natural disasters was more unrest in the Middle East causing the United States to partake in another Middle Eastern war. Beginning with a series of peaceful protests against the 41-year rule of Muammar Gaddafi in Libya, the dictator's forces confronted protestors on February 15th 2011 causing the uprising to spread across the country. Gaddafi responded with military force attempting to use censorship and blocking of communications to help his cause.

The conflict escalated with the rebels forming a coalition called the Transitional National Council based in Benghazi. The International Criminal Court warned Gaddafi and his government that they may be committing crimes against humanity. Then the United Nations then passed a resolution to freeze the assets of the dictator and ten members of his inner circle as well as restrict them from travel. A further resolution authorized UN members to enforce a no-fly zone over Libya which led to the March 19th intervention when a collection of states went in and destroyed Libyan air defences. To add to the craziness, uprisings were also taking place in Tunisia, Syria and Yemen.

What the…? Was the world about to implode? Oh well. It wasn't the end of the world. Only the end of the world is the end of the world and then there would be no world to worry about so what's the point?

World Happy Dance

I had no intentions of letting all the sadness in the world get me down. The last thing the world needed was another unhappy camper to add to the pool of despair. More determined than ever to stay positive, I met with Monique at our favourite coffee shop to discuss the possibility of having our own travel show. Travel never fails to make the two of us happy and we wanted to bring more of it into our lives and get paid to do it.

▲ *My World Happy Dance logo included a stick woman dancing inside a caution sign.*

We needed an angle that would distinguish us from the other travel shows and that's when I got the idea to make a show about the two of us happy dancing around the world.

How cool would that be to have footage of us busting a move at famous monuments and historical sites throughout the world?

I was so excited about the idea that I went home and created a website called .worldhappydance.com to track our progress. I spent the next day developing our logo, a stick person dancing inside a caution sign with the caption CAUTION HAPPY DANCE IN PROGRESS. I created a stick woman and a stick man because I believe happy dancing is for men and women.

A week later we started filming our first webisode and within ten days our story had made the local and provincial news I had no idea the world loved to happy dance as well.

I then went about putting our logo on t-shirts (with the help of my computer and some special iron on paper) and before you know it the happy dance had the makings of its own clothing line.

We met for coffee the day after our story aired on Global BC wearing our new attire and much to our surprise, people recognized us as the happy dance girls.

With all the bad news taking place in the world people were ready for some good news. People were ready to happy dance and I wanted to be there capturing all the action for my YouTube channel. Perhaps if I was lucky I could even make a living happy dancing my way around the world.

Wow, I had gone from disliking the majority of the world to wanting to happy dance with everyone in two short months. Was I becoming enlightened or was I going crazy? I didn't care, I was having the time of my life and that's all that really mattered.

See You Later Corby

When I got back to Kamloops on March 1st, I decided I would end my book on April 1st - a month later. I had no idea that would be the day of my friend Corby's memorial.

I knew Corby was reaching the end of her life when I volunteered to publish her poetry book. Multiple Sclerosis had destroyed her body taking away her ability to walk, talk and even feed herself. MS is an autoimmune condition in which the immune system attacks the central nervous system. The myelin sheath that surrounds the neurons becomes damaged and causes impairment in sensation, muscle weakness, difficulties with coordination, problems in speech and vision, fatigue, acute or chronic pain and depression amongst other symptoms. The disease affects people of all ages but mostly young adults. As of yet there is no cure

My friend Becky had worked with Corby and after discovering that I was a writer asked me if I could help publish her poetry book. It had always been a dream of Corby's but that dream was taken away when she gave a family friend $2000 to publish her book but instead he took the money and disappeared.

Corby's care aids managed to find me a typewritten copy of her manuscript and with the help of my mother, I entered the text into the computer then formatted the book adding my own pictures and the drawings a care aid had made for her.

I worked on it every night after work for two weeks. When I returned back home from my camp job in Fort McMurray I planned to surprise her with it.

I will never forget the day all of her friends gathered in the dining area of the care home and applauded as I presented Corby with the first copy of her book. Corby's face burst with tears of joy knowing her dream had come true. We all took turns reading poems from the book while Corby laughed and cried.

I never imagined that a few years later I would be sitting in the same room with the same people reading from the same book at Corby's memorial.

While I was sad she wasn't with us anymore I was happy that she was finally free.

Visiting my friends at the care home always gave me a renewed sense of gratitude for everything I have. These people never cease to amaze me with their positive outlook on life. They are all confined to wheelchairs and suffer from a host of disabilities but they are happy for the most part. I have a wonderful life, a fully functioning body and the freedom to travel around the world and I spend my time moping about depressed. What was wrong with me?

While I silently said "see you later" to Corby I put in a request for her to find me a publisher. I figured she would have some great contacts in her new home. Then I read aloud the poem I ended her book with – the one that always sends shivers down my spine.

▲ *A picture of Corby in her younger years adorns the cover of her poetry book.*

One Day

By Corby-Ann Fehr

One day there will be a book
I hope you can remember my name
Then you can have a little look

I can tell you how
It used to be
And in 30 seconds
You will see

I used to be so fast
Never a day went by
Where I didn't have a blast
Now I can't even bath

You see this is hard to handle
So I pray to God
And light a candle

What Happens in Machu Picchu

I guess this is where book seven of my Teresa the Traveler series ends and the next begins. I don't know if I found my soul mate in South as I had hoped, but I certainly found my soul and a new best friend in Monique.

Monique also reconnected with herself on our trip. While sitting in the restaurant at Machu Picchu she started chatting with one of the tour operators. That conversation planted a seed in her mind about what she would like to do and when she returned home she opened up her own tour company called Tours by Q. She offers mountain bike and guided tours of the Kamloops area as well as tours of British Columbia. Check out her website at www.toursbc.ca. Starting her own business gave her a renewed excitement about life and because she loves what she does I have no doubt she will be incredibly successful. In fact she already attracted a bike sponsor and a bike rack sponsor called Tuff Racks. Not bad for her first month in business.

I managed to finish this book during my first month back at home but still had no idea how I was going to pay the bills until my dreams of being a professional happy dancer become a reality.

As for the love front, things between Antonio and I fizzled out and we never talked after I got back. I have no idea what happened and why it ended but I realized that despite the fact I loved him, I was happier without him. He was hot and cold and what I really wanted was warm.

Despite the fact I had finally became comfortable in my own skin and no longer believed I needed a relationship to make me happy, I still hoped I would one day meet that perfect man for me. Perhaps I had already had. John and I continued to send each other letters through Facebook and he was planning to visit me in Canada that summer. Perhaps, unlike Las Vegas, what happens in Machu Picchu doesn't always stay there.

I guess only time will tell.

▲ *I had no idea while I was sitting on top of Machu Picchu posing for this picture how that day was about to change my life.*

References

Note: Most of the prices listed here are low season prices; they may go up in the spring and summer during the high tourist season.

Hotel Ambala
Cra. 5 No. 13- 46
Bogota, Columbia
Tel: 342 6384 – 341 2376
Single $36 US
www.hotelambala.com
Rooms include shower, warm water and free wireless internet. Pick up from airport also available at an extra charge.

Flying Dog Hostel Peru
280 Martir Olaya St. Miraflores
Lima, Peru
Tel: 4470673
Single $30US
www.flyingdogperu.com
flyingdoghostles@gmail.com
Singles, double and triple rooms available as well as dorm rooms. Common kitchen, lounge and pub. Free internet.

Flying Dog Hostel Peru
116 Melgar Street
Arequipa, Peru
Tel: (0051) 54-231163
Single $27US
www.flyingdogperu.com
flyingdoghostles@gmail.com
This former Arequipian mansion has been recently transformed into a top notch hostel complete with bar, kitchen, TV room and a beautiful courtyard around a water fountain. Single and double rooms are available as well as dorm rooms for those on a tighter budget.

Hoseria Suiza
Huacachina
Ica, Peru
Tel: (056) 238762
Single $27US
www.hosteria-suiza.com
hostsuiza@terr.com.pe
This hostel has an outdoor swimming pool and a common kitchen and is located on the lagoon in Huacachina. Price includes breakfast.

Hostel Curasi
Huacachina
Ica, Peru
Tel: (056) 216989 – 227682
Cell: 956946333
Single $20US
www.huacachinacurasi.com
reservations@huacachinacurasi.com
This quiet hostel has rooms located around a courtyard with an outdoor pool. Price includes breakfast.

▲ *The Hoseria Suiza in Huacachina, Peru had a pool in the courtyard and was surrounded by huge sand dunes.*

Hostel Oro Viejo
Jr. Callao No. 483
Nasca, Peru
Tel: 05652 3332
Single $25US
oro_viejo@terra.com.pe
www.hoteloroviejo.net
This quiet hostel has a pool and private bathrooms and comfortable beds. It is located 2 blocks from the bus station.

San Blas II
Hostal Turistico
Calle Choquechaca No. 194
Cusco, Peru
Tel: 051 (084) 22436
Cell: 984615747
Single $26US
sanblas2cusco@hotmail.com
www.hostalsanblas2.com
This is one of the best hostals in Cusco. It is located on a quiet street within walking distance of the main square and has great beds and a large newer common area.

Hotel Mundial
Avendia de Mayo, 1298
Buenos Aires, Argentina
Tel: 54 11 5254 0001
Single $53US
recepcion@mundialhotel.com.ar
www.mundialhotel.com.ar
Located in central Buenos Aires this hotel is simple and clean.

Colonial Iguazu
Iguazu, Argentina
Tel: (03757) 422898
Cell: (03757) 15461639
Single $38US
www.colonialiguazu.com
Hotel has a pool in the courtyard and shared kitchen. Single rooms overlooking the pool have no air-conditioning. Double rooms with air-conditioning cost $50

Hostel Natura
Misiones 32
Iguazu, Argentina
Single $50US
pophostelnatura@hotmail.com
www.hostelnaturaiguazu.com
Nice rooms with bathtubs, smoking is permitted throughout hotel.

Hotel Colonial
Zuviria 6 Plaza Principal
Salta, Argentina
Single $50US
hotelcolonial@salnet.com.ar
www.saltahotelcolonial.com.ar
The hotel offers bright, cozy rooms with bathtubs that overlook Plaza 9 de Julio with spacious common areas and friendly staff.

El Rincon
San Pedro, Chile
Licancabur
Singles $40 US
Don't expect much from this simple hostel where the bathrooms are shared but the showers are hot but it is a bargain in this pricey town.

Howard Johnson Maingate East
Kissimmee, Florida
6051 W Irlo Bronson Memorial Hwy. 192
Tel: 866-299-2910
Singles $25 US
www.hojomge.com
Free shuttles to Disney World, swimming pool and free internet in the lobby are all offered in this quiet hotel. It is also located within walking distance of grocery stores, restaurants and a Starbucks.

Hotel Kutimuy
Uyuni, Bolivia
Tel: 6932391
Singles $13US
This clean hotel with comfortable mattresses is a great bang for your buck.

Hotel Osira
La Paz, Bolivia
Av. 20 Octubre #1494
Plaza Mariscal Sucre (San Pedro)
Tel: (591) 2-2492247
Singles $40 US
ventas@hotelosira.com
www.hotelosira.com
This 3-star hotel offers warm showers, internet in the rooms, comfortable beds and television. Rooms at the front overlook San Pedro Plaza

Whitelaw Hotel
South Beach, Miami, Florida
808 Collins Avenue
Miami Beach, Florida, 33139
Tel: 305.398.7000
Singles $83 US
www.whitelawhotel.com
If you love the art-deco look this is the hotel for you. White washed rooms accented by red dots on the ceiling and mirrored tables make you want to say groovy baby. However, if you are looking for peace and quiet this is not the hotel for you as the lobby is a lounge that blasts out dance music from noon till late into the night and each room comes equipped with a stereo.

Continental Plaza Hotel
Kissimmee, Florida
7785 W. U.S. Hwy. 192
Tel: 407-396-1828
Singles $45 US
www.continentalplazahotel.com
This quiet hotel is the perfect home base for your Disneyworld adventure. Rooms have internet, TV, a fridge and a microwave. The hotel provides a free daily shuttle to and from the park and there are plenty of restaurants and amenities nearby.

Business Reference

Curasi Tours
Balneario de Huacachina
Ica, Peru
Tel: (056) 216989
Cell: 956946333
resercas@huacachinacurasi.com
www.huacachinacurasi.com
Sand dune buggy and boarding adventures for a great price.

Cruz del Sur
Peru
www.cruzdelsuri.com.pe
Comfortable air-conditioned secure buses offer first class and coach seating. Service includes a meal and free movies.

▲ Curasi Tours Balneario de Huacachina in Ica, Peru offer sand dune barding and sand buggy tours.

Cena Tango Show
Av. Belgrano 2608
Tel: 4941-1119
Tango classes and dinner theatre

Colque Tours
Caracoles Street and Calama Street
San Pedro, Chile
Tel: (0056) 92188728
www.colquetours.com
info@colquetours.com
Colque tours, one of many tour companies in San Pedro, provides no frills tours of Chile and Bolivia for the budget traveler.

La Terraza Cafe
Av. 16 de Julio #1615
La Paz, Bolivia
This trendy well run café chain serves the best mocha lattes and pita pizzas ever!

Mears Motor Shuttle
Tel: 407-423-5566
Orlando, Florida
Mears is your best option for getting from your hotel to the airport as they are much cheaper than a taxi.

Recommended Books

Lonely Planet, *South America on a Shoestring*, 2007

101 Great Wonders of the World, 2007, AA Publishing, printed by Oriental Press in Dubai

The Traveler's Atlas, John Man and Chris Schuler, 2004, Quatro Inc. Barron's Educational Series, Hauppauge, New York

501 Must-See Natural Wonders, Poly Manguel, 2007, Great Britian

Recommended Websites

www.wikipedia.com

www.travelocity.com

www.hotels.com

www.expedia.com

Purchase your
E-book or print copy at
www.teresathetravler.com

Or contact Teresa the
Traveler at:
teresathetraveler@hotmail.com

www.ingramcontent.com/pod-product-compliance
Ingram Content Group UK Ltd.
Pitfield, Milton Keynes, MK11 3LW, UK
UKHW020130250726
13967UKWH00002B/563